W9-AHW-463

Soothing Moments
Daily Meditations
For Fast-Track Living

Bryan E. Robinson, Ph.D.

Health Communications, Inc.
Deerfield Beach, Florida

DEDICATION

To Phyllis Henline for her courage and inspiration and all the love and joy she has given to so many people.

© 1990 Bryan E. Robinson
ISBN 1-55874-075-9

Publisher: Health Communications, Inc.
         3201 S.W. 15th Street
         Deerfield Beach, Florida 33442

INTRODUCTION

The daily meditations in this book are for super-achievers who are doing too much and finding themselves overly stressed and out of touch with their spirituality. Many of us put everything and everyone else in life before ourselves: our jobs, our relationships, our families, our friends. Caught up in the frantic pace of today's world, we are speed-reading, quick-fixing, rush-houring, fast-tracking and hustling and bustling ourselves to death. Co-dependent lifestyles whip us into frenzied submission as we try to please others, to do things perfectly, to never say no and always to put our own needs last.

Job and family commitments are overwhelming; there is never any time for us. When we live our lives for others, there is so much to do and so little time in which to complete it. Stress and burnout are high, hence we become frustrated, irritable and impatient because of our inability to accomplish these inhuman tasks and to slow down even when we are willing.

We will learn through these daily meditations that we cannot be all things to all people. Even if we live every day of the year trying to be what everyone wants us to be, at some point we will disappoint or anger someone. We can find fulfillment only by knowing, caring for and loving ourselves first. We learn the true joy in taking some time each day for self-renewal and self-replenishment.

These daily readings will help us break through the bonds of co-dependency, high-pressured lifestyles and chronic overdoing. The meditations guide us through each day of the year with hope and optimism, teaching us to live our lives with serenity. They show us how to empower ourselves to create happy, fulfilling and balanced lives. They help us achieve balance by discovering the inner anchor that keeps us secure and unwavering in the fast-paced sea in which we swim daily. We discover that we are not alone and that we have the 12 Steps, prayer, meditations and our Higher Power to guide our spiritual process of breaking through the bonds of overachieving, fast-track living and chronic stress day by day and one step at a time.

Bryan Robinson

"We shall not cease from exploration
And the end of all our exploring
Will be to arrive where we started
And know the place for the first time."

T.S. Eliot

Today we turn over a new leaf on our journey of self-exploration, which begins as we awaken spiritually like sleepy children. We admit that we are powerless over our fast track living and that our lives have become unmanageable. We heal our lives by looking within for spiritual strength that comes day by day and one step at a time. We are uncertain but gradually we wake up and feel centered, grounded and self-confident. We are ready to embrace each day on our spiritual path.

Today I acknowledge that my fast-paced, co-dependent lifestyle has made my life unmanageable. Having chosen the path of spiritual exploration, I let my Higher Power choose my destination.

"For of all sad words of tongue or pen, the saddest are these: 'It might have been!'"

John Greenleaf Whittier

The following anonymous quotation also addresses this point: "If I had my life to live over, I would have talked less and listened more. I would have invited friends over even though the carpet was stained and the sofa was faded. I would have burned the candle sculpted like a rose before it melted in storage. I would have gone to bed when I was sick instead of worrying that the earth would go into a holding pattern if I missed work. There would have been more 'I love you,' more 'I am sorry.'"

Today I live my life so that if someone asks me, "If you had your life to live over, what would you change?" My answer would be, "Not one single thing!"

"A man who trims himself to suit everybody will soon whittle himself away."

Charles Schwab

A major truth in life: Someone will be mad or displeased with us. Trying to appease everyone only brings us misery and whittles us down until there's nothing left.

Healing comes when we realize no one has taken advantage of us. We have *let* them take advantage of us. The solution to this is to live our lives to please ourselves. We will feel better about ourselves because we have become our own person. Being in touch with who we are helps us love and care for ourselves and then we are in a better position to love and care for others.

Today I live my life to suit me. I love myself first and give myself the same respect that I give to others.

"The more a human being feels himself a self, tries to intensify this self and reach a never attainable perfection, the more drastically he steps out of the center of being . . ."

Eugene Herrigel

Those of us who are co-dependent often depend on accomplishments for our self-esteem. When recognition doesn't come, we feel worthless. Recovery comes as we learn to accept ourselves, regardless of the messages we get from the outside world. Self-affirmations help us recognize our beauty and worth.

Today my worth doesn't depend on everyone liking me. Things do not have to be perfect for me to be happy. I forgive myself for my imperfections and accept myself as I am.

"They intoxicate themselves with work so they won't see how they really are."

Aldous Huxley

Those of us who work compulsively suffer some of the same co-dependent symptoms as alcoholics. We are just as powerless over our need to work as drug addicts are over their substance of choice. Although work abuse draws applause, it destroys relationships and can even cause death.

Once we discover that work addiction is not a positive addiction, we can learn the difference between abusive work and healthy work. We can heal ourselves from overworking by committing ourselves to a spiritual life.

Today I heal my life by connecting with my spiritual self. All other parts of my life will fall into place.

"The man who saves time by galloping loses it by missing his way . . . economy does not consist in haste, but in certainty."

J. Ramsay MacDonald

For some of us life is one crisis after another. We create conflict in our lives when we get too many irons in the fire, overschedule or set unrealistic deadlines. Our lives become unmanageable because we try to run them without help. Just when we think it's hopeless, we turn our lives over to our Higher Power who gives us tranquility.

Today I avoid crisis by refraining from overdoing, overorganizing and overscheduling. Instead, I pace myself for my own serenity and for the sake of friends, family and colleagues.

"To err is human, to forgive, divine."

Alexander Pope

Some of us feel compelled to generate lists and, as we check each item off, we feel gratified with the completion. If we fall short of our goals — no matter how unreasonable they may be — we torture ourselves by putting ourselves down and making ourselves feel worthless.

Learning to forgive ourselves is a true measure of success. As long as we can forgive ourselves, we are never defeated. Everyone falls short at one time or another and failure is a natural part of being human.

Today I accept my shortcomings with my triumphs and when I fail, I forgive myself, release my negative self-doubts and allow myself to be human.

"Patience is the best remedy for every trouble."

Plautus

When we have lived our lives in co-dependent relationships for so long, we must be patient as we begin the recovery process. It has taken us years to get into our present fix, and we cannot expect to undo the negative patterns in one day, week or even a month. Impatience in recovery sabotages our spiritual growth. Recovery doesn't happen on our time schedules while spiritual growth evolves gradually as a process.

Today I am patient and confident in my spiritual growth. Changing my life will not occur on my time schedule. My spiritual growth is totally guided by my Higher Power, who knows what is best for me at all times.

"Golden hours of vision come to us in this present life when . . . our faculties work together in harmony."

C.F. Dole

Healthy people work in order to live, but others of us live in order to work. Our lives become unbalanced because everything is neglected in favor of work. First we must admit we are powerless and second believe that a Power greater than us can restore serenity. Taking time to develop a balance in our lives will ensure harmony within ourselves, at work and at play. Our jobs are only one part of our lives.

Today I seek balance. Only through interaction with friends and loved ones and inner reflection can I find self-fulfillment.

"The bluebird carries the sky on his back."

Henry David Thoreau

How many of us bite off more than we can chew? Do we refuse to share the workload, then complain that we are overworked? In the hustle and bustle of the everyday world it is possible to build our emotions into a crescendo of jealousy, competitiveness and greed.

No matter how burdened we feel, we can lift our spirits by the mental attitudes we take.

Today I release all my negative thoughts and feelings. I am filled with positive thoughts, feelings and behaviors that return to me through the generosity, love and kindness of those with whom I interact.

"I have plumbed the depths of despair and have found them not bottomless."

Thomas Hardy

Our greatest achievements come from our greatest pain. Sometimes it takes reaching our lowest point before we are ready to begin our spiritual transformation. Just when we feel we can fall no lower and our situation is hopeless, a miracle happens. We fall up, not down. We fall into recovery and see the way out of our predicament.

Belief in a Higher Power restores us with hope when we are down. When all else is gone, the Higher Power is always there.

Today I experience more happiness and fulfillment than I ever thought possible. Today I feel my Higher Power guiding me through the mist and into the light.

"The foolish reject what they see, not what they think; the wise reject what they think, not what they see."

Huang Po

With the help of our Higher Power, all of us have choices we can make about our lives. The past can never be fully erased but its effects can be altered. No matter how horrendous our yesterdays we can transform them into meaningful and fulfilling todays and tomorrows.

When bad things happen to us, we do not view them as roadblocks but as stepping stones which lead us to a higher quality of life.

Today I transform the negative into the positive. I ask myself, "What in my life can I change that will help me and others to live a fuller, more meaningful life?"

"It does not matter how slowly you go as long as you do not stop."

Confucius

Recovery from any form of co-dependency is a process, not an end result. We never truly arrive anywhere on the road of recovery. But we are always getting better and better during our journey, and the quality of our lives is always improving.

We can feel ourselves getting healthier and happier, day by day and one step at a time as we put our trust in our Higher Power. Reminding ourselves that important things take time helps us to be patient with the process.

Today I give myself credit for the tiny gains I make in my growth. I know that these small steps eventually add up to giant leaps.

"Humanity is never so beautiful as when praying for forgiveness or else forgiving another."

Jean Paul Richter

Families of compulsive workers suffer too. In evaluating our own excessive working and fast-track living, we begin to see how loved ones become co-dependent by getting caught up in our chaos. One way in which we deal with those whom we have hurt is to make a list of all persons we have harmed, and become willing to make amends. Taking this step can help us think about how our actions affect those we care about. This simple act puts us back in touch with our humanity and helps us grow spiritually.

Today I conduct myself to the best of my ability and treat others with love and respect. I am totally willing to make amends to all persons I have harmed.

"*. . . It is when tomorrow's burden is added to the burden of today that the weight is more than a man can bear.*"

George MacDonald

When we become swamped with our jobs, family responsibilities and trying to maintain a social life, it is sometimes more than we can bear. We become short-tempered, forgetful and tired. When we feel overburdened and burned out, we can turn our lives and our will over to a Higher Power. This Power leads us through the stressful times and restores our sanity. Calm descends upon us as we begin to face one day at a time.

Today I allot a segment of time to center my thoughts and feelings and connect with my inner self. My Higher Power gives me the strength to weather any storm.

"The excuse that thou dost make in this delay is longer than the tale thou dost excuse."

William Shakespeare

We often use excuses for co-dependent living. We say we stay busy out of loyalty to our employers or to provide a decent living. Staying busy medicates our emotional pain and protects us from intimacy with others. Only by understanding and admitting the real reasons behind our co-dependent lifestyles can we find peace and happiness. We can now allow ourselves to feel our stored emotions without numbing them with work and the need for excuses will melt away.

Today I offer no excuses for excessive busyness because they are only excuses. I allow myself to feel my emotions fully and to experience the healing process.

"His only fault is that he has no fault."

Pliny The Younger

Many of us are such sticklers that nobody, not even ourselves, can meet our standards of perfection. Our way is the only way.

When we turn our lives and our wills over to a Higher Power, we receive the gift of humility and are able to release ourselves and others from unrealistic expectations. We learn that each person is different and our way is only one way out of many.

Today I allow the people in my life to be and to express themselves in ways that are natural to them. I give myself permission to make mistakes. I open myself to the creative approaches, ideas and behaviors of others and am willing to learn from them.

"Temperance and industry are man's true remedies; work sharpens his appetite and temperance teaches him to control it."

Jean Jacques Rousseau

We cannot simply stop working but we find as we do cut down and spread our time lines out over longer time frames that we become more effective at what we do. We feel less stressed, have fewer physical ailments, and feel more harmony with our families and ourselves. Spiritual healing helps us practice moderation in work and in all other areas of our lives.

Today I am practicing abstinence in all areas of my life. I am no longer enslaved by my work schedule. I am broadening myself spiritually and socially and spending quality time with loved ones.

"For how many things, which our own sake we should never do, do we perform for the sake of our friends."

Marcus Tullius Cicero

Many of us go through life rescuing other people from life. We are attracted to friends and lovers, even business associates, for whom we feel sorry. Rescuing keeps the focus off of us and on someone else. We may hear a lecture and think, "Now this is what my spouse or friend needs to hear." We spend so much time saving others that we neglect ourselves and miss opportunities for our own growth. The recovery process teaches us to rescue ourselves and love and care for ourselves.

Today I am rescuing me. I am not distracted by rescuing co-workers, loved ones and friends who need someone to take care of their needs for them.

"Consciousness is always open to many possibilities because it involves play. It is always an adventure."

Julian Jaynes

Sometimes we are so overly serious that we think it is irresponsible to take a lighter approach to life. Too many of us have forgotten how to have fun. The lighter side of life gives us relief from daily pressures. All of us have a playful child inside, longing to come out. Spiritual healing is not all grim determination; it occurs through lighthearted fun too.

Today I will make a special effort to lighten up. I will release my inner child by looking on the bright side and inviting humor and play as my companions.

"More men are killed by overwork than the importance of the work justifies."

Rudyard Kipling

Co-dependent personalities are not born; they are molded by dysfunctional family experiences. We overachieve in everything. These survival patterns helped us get through our childhood but when we carry our super-child syndrome into adulthood, it destroys our lives.

On a spiritual path we willingly let go of the course of self-destruction we have been on since childhood and vow our family's dysfunction will stop here.

Today I will name all the self-destructive behaviors I have clutched to survive my past. One by one I will let them go.

"Do they miss me at home — do they miss me? 'Twould be an assurance most dear, to know that this moment some loved one were saying, 'I wish he were here.' "

Caroline Atherton Briggs Mason

Grueling work demands sometimes cause us to neglect our families. Our kids and spouses beg for our attention and we resent their *intrusions* because we are already overcommitted. Children of chronic overachievers are literally orphans and spouses are single parents. We can evaluate our priorities in life and ask forgiveness for the loved ones we have neglected.

Today I cherish the ones who lovingly took a back seat while work sat up front with me. Beginning now I give my loved ones the equal time they deserve.

"Rehearsal is a period of time to make mistakes. Only by practicing over and over do we learn the new and make it a natural part of us."

Louise Hay

Acting in the theater requires flexibility. In rehearsals, scenes are frequently changed. No one expects perfection the first time around. Life is a dress rehearsal. How can we be perfect at something we've never done before? The universe and the rules by which it operates are perfect. Human beings are not. We are still learning our lines. This is what spiritual growth is all about.

Today everyone I know, myself included, is still in rehearsal. Colleagues, friends and family members will make mistakes and so will I. All is forgiven before I face today's cast of characters.

"All numbers are multiples of one, all sciences converge to a common point, all wisdom comes out of one center, and the number of wisdom is one."

Paracelsus

How many of us feel incomplete and unfinished? We fill up this void by stuffing our lives with projects but they never do and never will bring self-fulfillment. Recovery comes from the discovery that we already have all that is necessary to be complete, one is a whole number. We do not need work on another person as we need only to tap into the spiritual flow of our Higher Power.

Today I do not need my work or another person to make me feel complete. I am whole just as I am. My relationship with my Higher Power helps me to feel this wholeness more and more with each new day.

"No one is injured save by himself."

Desiderius Erasmus

Many of us have been told through actions or words that we are not important. Some of us become emotional invalids when we allow old thoughts to paralyze us. We spend our lives figuring out what others want us to be like and our interests and goals change to match those of the people we are with at the moment. Feelings of importance come from within. We must believe we count for something and once we feel that we are worthy of respect, people will start to treat us with respect.

Today I ask in what ways I have made myself an emotional invalid. I count for something, and I will feel and behave in accordance with this thought.

"Responsibility's like a string we can only see the middle of. Both ends are out of sight."

William McFee

All of us have certain responsibilities to meet, but an overdeveloped sense of responsibility makes us feel responsible for everyone and everything around us. When we become overly responsible, we become enmeshed in co-dependent relationships. We rob our partner of an opportunity to be responsible and we contribute to our own burnout. We are responsible for our own behavior and happiness and others are responsible for theirs.

Today I distinguish responsibility from overresponsibility. I relinquish my urge to take responsibility for others that would rob them of their growth and deprive me of mine.

*"An essential inner need has been satisfied,
and against that satisfaction, that self-fulfillment, no external power can prevail."*

Antoine de Saint Exupéry

A writer submitted an article to a magazine
for publication. Going about her daily life, she
was happier than ever. Then she received a
letter rejecting her manuscript. Suddenly she
was hurled into a deep depression. Do we put
our emotional well-being at the mercy of one
incident in our daily lives? Drawing from our
inner strength, however, will keep our feet
planted on the ground when disappointments
try to uproot us.

*Today when I count my blessings, I see
that I have much more to be thankful for
than to fret about. Life is full of disappointments but I choose to experience them as
lessons that build inner fortitude.*

"In order to be utterly happy the only thing necessary is to refrain from comparing this moment with other moments in the past, which I often did not fully enjoy because I was comparing them with other moments of the future."

André Gide

Many of us remember a time when we have been hurt. The betrayal of a colleague, the abuse of a parent. It may have happened last week or ten years ago but the pain is still there. Unresolved hurts are like an invisible wall that says, "Keep Out!" to those around us. They only harm one person — the one carrying them around. Once we face inner hurts, horrible things do not happen. We heal.

Today I ask myself what pain am I still carrying around. I process these old hurts and allow healing to begin.

"*. . . How much easier it is to be critical than to be correct.*"

Benjamin Disraeli

The tongue is a powerful and sharp sword that can cut, disfigure, cripple and even kill the human spirit. We can do more damage to others and to ourselves with hateful comments than with a nuclear bomb. But kind words, loving affirmations and affectionate support can do more to soothe and mend an injured spirit than any human medicine.

Do we use our tongues to condemn or do we use our voices to uplift, heal and support?

Today I am ever mindful that my words can harm or heal. I choose what I say to myself and others carefully. I use my words to comfort and heal rather than to injure.

"Men are disturbed not by things, but by the views which they take of them."

Epictetus

It is not what life deals us that determines our happiness or unhappiness; it's our perceptions and reactions to what life deals us that determine our happiness. If we view ourselves as empowered and use life's disadvantages to learn and improve our own lives, then we create a positive experience out of a negative one. We are powerless to control our lives, but we receive power from our Higher Power who is always there for us. When we have faith in this Power, we live with happiness and fulfillment.

Today I am not a victim of life's circumstances. I am a survivor of them. I choose to view my life with hope and optimism for the future.

"We believe that everything there is to find is out there in the light where it's easy to find, when the only answers for you *are in* you*!"*

Leo Buscaglia

We search frantically for purpose in our daily lives expecting our work to provide fulfillment or another person to make us complete. We look in the wrong place when we search outside ourselves for purpose in life. We discover it when we look within and connect with a Power greater than ourselves. The word "guru" is spelled "Gee-You-Are-You." Inner happiness, peace and contentment come when we look within for the answers.

Today I look within myself for answers to my spiritual quest. I know that through the divine inspiration of my Higher Power spiritual fulfillment is mine.

"The more a man is united within himself, and interiorly simple, the more and higher things doth he understand without labour; because he receiveth the light of understanding from above."

Thomas à Kempis

We fly solo "so low" when we use our self-will to force our lives to go the way we want. On our own we can never know all that is needed to keep us aloft. But belief in a Power greater than ourselves helps us soar. When we allow our Higher Power to navigate, we face each day with renewed faith and courage. It gives us the inner strength to overcome any obstacles and serenity is ours.

Today I no longer fly solo. I am Higher Powered with wings to soar in my spiritual search.

"And so it criticized each flower, this supercilious seed; until it woke one summer hour, and found itself a weed."

Mildred Howells

"I should have remembered that appointment;" "I should have done better in that tennis game." The word "should" could easily be eliminated from our vocabulary because it implies that nothing is ever good enough. All of us have strengths that, when combined, make a beautiful bouquet but no single flower can be the entire bouquet. We cannot be all things to all people but we can be the best that we can be.

Today I acknowledge the beauty of my own flower, I replace the word "should" with "could" and give myself choices, not condemnation.

"The victory, joy and growth aren't achieved by avoiding. The rewards come by overcoming. Each time we surrender and let go, we'll be propelled forward on our journey."

Melody Beattie

Those of us who are chronic caretakers feel responsible for whatever happens around us. Our recovery comes from surrender — from realizing we cannot control anyone or anything but ourselves and that we can be responsible only for ourselves. As we allow ourselves to be human with all its fallibilities and strengths, we practice the art of self-care.

Today I know that I can only take care of myself. It is everyone else's responsibility to take care of themselves and I am not at fault if things go wrong.

"Holidays should be like this, free from over-emphasis, time for the soul to stretch and spit before the world comes back on it."

Louis MacNeice

Celebrations and holidays are the glue that holds families together. It is important to take time out to acknowledge them because co-dependent lifestyles often cause us to miss important celebrations as we busy ourselves to do for others. We feel emptiness, guilt and hurt looking back over the times that we hurried through. Once missed, they are gone forever. We are worth celebrating and our lives are worth celebrating.

Today I will celebrate the rituals in my life with vigor and enthusiasm and I will celebrate my new life on the road of spiritual awareness.

"Our life is like some vast lake that is slowly filling with the stream of our years. As the waters creep surely upward the landmarks of the past are one by one submerged. But there shall always be memory to lift its head above the tide until the lake is overflowing."

Alexandre Charles Auguste Bisson

We often blame our present misery on our dysfunctional past but yesterday is gone forever. Spiritual progress begins when we can change how we look at our past, then we can begin to see old destructive events as opportunities for growth.

Today I cannot change yesterday or control tomorrow but I can live now to the fullest. I accept today and make the best of every moment that I have in it.

"The only thing we have to fear is fear itself."

Franklin D. Roosevelt

Our high levels of perfection come from a deep-seated fear of inadequacy, failure, rejection and abandonment. Our fear of failure becomes a self-fulfilling prophecy which ruins our physical and emotional health and cripples our relationships with others. Fear of failing is a feeling that can be changed by our mental outlook on life. We can willingly give up our fears of failing and rejection by loving ourselves unconditionally.

Today I do not stand in the way of my own success as a human being. I love and accept myself unconditionally and release myself and others from the chains of inhuman perfection.

"A pessimist is one who makes difficulties of his opportunities; an optimist is one who makes opportunities of his difficulties."

Reginald B. Mansell

No one is truly helpless. That's simply a negative way of thinking that allows us to be victims of life. There are some things over which we have no control, for example, the actions of others, our addictions, the tides. But with divine support we are never helpless over our own thoughts, feelings and behaviors. We ask our Higher Power to give us the strength to change the helpless ways we think and feel about ourselves.

Today I am in charge. No matter what happens, I receive spiritual support to determine how I think, feel and behave. I accept responsibility for my own actions.

"No one can make you feel inferior without your consent."

Eleanor Roosevelt

We waste a lot of time and energy berating others. As long as we blame other people or situations for our problems we prevent ourselves from accepting the responsibility for changing our lives for the better. The solutions to our problems are not outside ourselves; they reside within. When we stop blaming other people, we come a long way in our spiritual growth. Once we accept responsibility for our lives, they start to improve.

Today with the help of my Higher Power I accept responsibility for my life and vow to cleanse my mind of resentments and harmful thoughts and to love myself above all else.

"Every man is the builder of a temple, called his body."

                Henry David Thoreau

When we are on the go, we do not always keep our minds and bodies in top shape. We grab fast foods and forget to rest and exercise. Eventually, emotional and physical health problems start to surface. We ignore aches and pains that could be dangerous or even lead to death.

We can pay attention to our body messages as they can enable us to take proper steps to have them checked. Responding to ourselves with love and attention provides us the spiritual nurturance to heal the mind and body.

Today I shower myself with healthy caring and concern. I am reminded that recovery includes healing not only mind and spirit but also the body.

"Every moment that I am centered in the future, I suffer a temporary loss of this life."

Hugh Prather

We rush to work, rush to get afternoon errands done, hurry home to meet kids or prepare meals and rush to complete household chores. We never seem to have time left for ourselves. As we slow down and pay attention to the now, we are in touch with our lives and ourselves in the present.

Today I complete ME by carving out some quiet time to attune to my inner needs. I am filled with peace and tranquility and replenished to begin a new day.

"Nature does abhor a vacuum, and when you begin moving out of your life what you do not want, you automatically are making way for what you do want."

Catherine Ponder

Harboring anger, hate and discontent leaves no room for love, happiness and contentment. Like athletes we keep ourselves spiritually fit by releasing unhealthy thoughts and feelings that block our path. We create an inner vacuum by ridding ourselves of harmful feelings and making room for positive ones.

Today I create an inner vacuum. I evacuate all the self-defeating thoughts and feelings that I have stored in my mind. I refill the vacuum with healthy thoughts and feelings to take the place of the old, worn-out ones.

"Our problem is not that we take refuge from action in spiritual things, but that we take refuge from spiritual things in action."

Monica Furlong

Getting caught up in today's rat race requires that we wear many hats and we become filled with anxiety, anger, sadness and frustration. However, we do not have to get caught up in the volume of responsibilities that we have created in our lives because when conflicts arise, we can turn them over to a Power greater than ourselves, instead of taking them out on innocent bystanders.

Today I look for solutions to performing the many difficult roles in my life without hurting innocent loved ones. I call on my Higher Power for the clarity, serenity and inner strength to face these challenges.

"Gratitude is the sign of noble souls."

Aesop

The children need a new pair of shoes, the house needs a new roof and the dishwasher is broken. We can rant and rave about our needs and wants so much that we forget to be grateful for the things we have.

How many times a day do we stop and give thanks for the blessings we do have? Our family has their health, we have plenty of food on the table, we have each other, we're alive and we have a roof over our heads. We have this day and we have our Higher Power.

Today I will be conscious of all the wonderful blessings in my life. I will not complain about what I need but I will express gratitude for all the riches that I already have.

"No one is injured save by himself."

Desiderius Erasmus

When we make a list of all the people we have harmed and become willing to make amends to them all, we must remember to put ourselves at the top of the list. Unless we love ourselves, we can never love or help another person. When we love ourselves first and foremost, we transfer that self-love into caring for and helping those around us. Thinking back over the day, we can credit ourselves with all we have learned and the creative ways we have handled difficult situations. As we practice self-love, it spills over into our goodwill toward everyone in our lives.

Today I love myself and do good things for me. My self-love is automatically transferred to others.

"*We believe that according to our desire we are able to change the things round about us . . . we do not succeed in changing things according to our desire, but gradually our desire changes.*"

Marcel Proust

We often overreact to changes over which we have no control and struggle to manage everyone and everything around us. No human being is powerful enough to eliminate the unexpected, no matter how well organized they are. The only foolproof plan is to leave predicting, consistency and control to a Higher Power and then fear of losing control is replaced with tranquility and flexibility.

Today I give up the fear of losing control of my life. I am not the controller of my life anyway; my Higher Power is. As I turn my life over to this Greater Power, my fears evaporate.

"*If you wish to travel far and fast, travel light. Take off all your envies, jealousies, unforgiveness, selfishness and fears.*"

Glenn Clark

Much of our emotional pain comes from unresolved hurts that we carry from the past into the present and we often spend our lives reacting emotionally from old hurts rather than acting from the present experience. We can begin to take stock in the emotional baggage that we carry around and leave behind the worn-out feelings, repacking only the ones that are useful to us on our spiritual journey.

Today I unpack old emotional pain and deal with it now. As I continue on my spiritual road, my load is a little lighter and my step a little quicker.

*"Beware of desp'rate steps! The darkest day
'live till tomorrow' will have pass'd away."*

William Cowper

Some days are full of anxiety, frustration and irritability. These are the difficult times that accompany recovery. Sometimes we have to take three steps backward before leaping ten steps forward but falling back is part of moving forward. Being lonely, sad and tense are normal human feelings that everyone has from time to time. Knowing that these too shall pass gives us hope for tomorrow and strength to endure today.

Today when I feel like giving up, I remember that these days are part of the recovery process. I will accept the lows with the highs and experience them as fodder for my spiritual nourishment.

"We are healed of a suffering only by experiencing it to the full."

Marcel Proust

Changing our lives is risky business. It takes courage to restructure our lives from old ways to new ones. It doesn't come easy, and it doesn't come fast. Courage takes effort and patience. Being courageous means having faith that we've chosen the best path. Trusting in a greater Power to guide us and handle all outcomes is another form of courage. Courage has a healing effect because it helps us face and experience our lives to the fullest — no matter what happens.

Today I will be courageous in all decisions that I must make. I will make changes that bring me peace and fulfillment when and where I can.

"We have not managed to surmount the obstacle . . . but life has taken us round it . . . and then if we turn round to gaze at the remote past, we can barely catch sight of it . . ."

Marcel Proust

A woman's husband had left her with no money and two small children. She was at her wits' end so she prayed and felt she was being told to get busy and do something. She decided to clean her bedroom where she found an envelope with five $100 bills inside. She had forgotten she had put them there years before.

While many of us worry about how we will surmount problems, life often takes us around them. Faith in miracles frees us from needless worry.

Today I have faith that miracles in my life will work without wondering how and when they will happen. I leave that up to my Higher Power.

"Her mask is impenetrable now. Inside her breasts there are volcanoes smouldering. Do you think we can reach her before she explodes?"

Ruth Gendler

After years of hurt, we wear masks to prevent others from seeing our true selves and feeling our own feelings. Eventually, we lose touch with ourselves altogether. We can look behind our mask and ask ourselves what feelings we find there. As we face our feelings with honesty, we come to understand ourselves in a way that we never have before. We grow and we feel fully human.

Today I take one stone down from the wall I have built. Day by day, as I become emotionally stronger and stronger, I will remove the wall stone by stone. I embrace the self that is revealed to me.

"Humility is the truth about ourselves loved."

C. Carey-Elwes

Without humility there is no progress in recovery. Being humble, we admit who we truly are with both our strengths and frailties. Humility is not the same as humiliation. We do not make ourselves doormats on which other people wipe their feet. Being humble means surrendering to the positive energy of the universe, not the negative energy of those who would do us harm. In humility we retain our self-respect, while admitting our human imperfections and our need for a Power greater than ourselves.

Today I divorce myself from self-ridicule and false pride. I open myself to truth, clarity, soundness of mind and inner peace.

"Once the realization is accepted that even between the closest human beings infinite distances continue to exist, a wonderful living side by side can grow up, if they succeed in loving the distance between them which makes it possible for each to see the other whole against the sky."

Rainer Maria Rilke

Sometimes the negativity of others seems to pull us down. When people or situations become too much for us, we can detach ourselves while maintaining our love for them. Through the power of detachment we are able to continue to radiate joy and peace.

Today I do not take on the problems and negativity of my associates and loved ones but my compassion and love for their welfare is unyielding.

"We are the wire, God is the current. Our only power is to let the current pass through us."

Carlo Carretto

Children who break their toys give them to their parents to be repaired. Once the toy is fixed, the children want them back. In some ways we are like children with broken toys when we have problems. We wait before we are willing to surrender them to our Higher Power. Once our lives are running smoothly again, we snatch the controls back. As we grow spiritually we surrender and work on ourselves in a responsible way. Our Higher Power is our permanent guide.

Today I give up the urge to snatch the controls of my life, even when it is working. I remind myself that it is running smoothly because of my Higher Power.

*"Care to our coffin adds a nail, no doubt,
And every grin so merry draws one out."*

John Wilcot

Nutritionists tell us that we are what we eat. Eating well balanced meals keeps us healthy. Poor diets contribute to poor health. Spiritual nourishment works the same way. We are what we think. We can put healthy, positive thoughts into our minds and surround ourselves with spiritually fit people who support and affirm us. As our thinking becomes healthier and our feedback more enlightened, we reach greater harmony with life.

Today I purge my mind of all junk food. I avoid people who minimize my value and detract from my spiritual progress. I nourish my mind with a steady diet of healing thoughts and the company of affirming people.

"Every man has two journeys to make through life. There is the outer journey, with its various incidents and the milestones . . . There is also an inner journey, a spiritual odyssey, with a secret history of its own."

William R. Inge

We are on a spiritual odyssey that teaches us to know, love and care for ourselves. Our spiritual development becomes just as integral as work and family as we begin to include it in our daily lives. When we are in contact with our spiritual selves, the need for approval from others is replaced with self-affirmations.

Today I am not sleepwalking through my life. I am wide awake with spiritual knowing from my Higher Power that keeps me alert and assured of my direction.

"Make haste slowly."

Augustus

All of us have times when we feel so over-burdened and overwhelmed with problems that we cannot go on. Inside, we feel deeply unhappy and depressed and have lost all meaning for living. We can never solve all our problems at once but we can work them through day by day and one at a time. The Latin phrase *festina lente* is translated "make haste slowly." It means to move cautiously and step by step as we make changes in our lives. Facing one day at a time builds into weeks and months and we have accomplished much.

Today I will tackle only the things that demand resolution now. Tomorrow I will deal with tomorrow. Next week I will think about next week.

"Drones make more noise than bees, but all they make is the wax, not the honey. Those who torment themselves with eagerness and anxiety do little, and that badly."

St. Francis de Sales

Many of our stresses are mental attitudes that we have about situations, not the situations themselves. Once we gain awareness of how we react to stress, we can control how stressful we become. We don't have to get annoyed with colleagues who move at a snail's pace. From them we can learn to slow down. We can marvel at the uniqueness of our fellow human beings while realizing there are many ways to accomplish our ends.

Today I will look at how I create stress in my life. I will take stressful reactions and turn them into healthy and constructive actions that yield positive outcomes for myself and those around me.

"After all it is those who have a deep and real inner life who are best able to deal with the 'irritating details of outer life.' "

Evelyn Underhill

Nobody sails smoothly on the lake every-time out in a sailboat. Sometimes there's no wind and other times there's too much turbulence. Spiritual progress is like sailing a ship. We learn to adapt to life around us. We welcome with open arms temptation with triumph, sadness with joy and pain with pleasure. Faith in our Higher Power steers us through the storms and the calm.

Today I have wind in my sails. It may be too calm to move far or it may be so turbulent that I swirl in circles. But I adjust to the direction and force of the wind that blows my way.

"There is great fret and worry always running after work; it is not good intellectually or spiritually."

Annie Keary

Overdoing and fast-track living come in many packages that can do great harm to body, mind and spirit. Most people express these compulsive behaviors through their jobs but others express them through housework, raising kids, gardening or decorating. Replacing the need for busy lives with a rich spiritual life can heal compulsively busy habits.

Today I know that giving up a high-pressured job does not rid me of fast-track living. I can heal myself of compulsive work habits by balancing my life with a rich inner spiritual life.

"It is a sign of strength, not of weakness, to admit that you don't know all the answers."

John P. Loughrane

Turning our will and life over to the care of a Higher Power means many things. We let go of self-will and we willingly let our Higher Power unlock the closed door of our self-determination. We relinquish our omnipotence and admit that we do not know all the answers. When we turn our will over, we do not shirk our responsibilities or give up effort or self-discipline. We merely turn the guidance of our lives over to a Higher Knowing, who speaks to us in many ways.

Today I turn my will and life over to the care of my Higher Power. I do not give up my responsibilities or efforts but I am guided in them by a greater Knowing.

"Our hope is even livelier than despair, our joy livelier and more abiding than our sorrows are."

Robert Bridges

Living in co-dependency, whether as a child or a spouse, can be very difficult. Everybody in the family is affected by the experience and some of the dysfunctional habits are passed on to the children. The cycle can stop with us. We do not hold other family members to the same old thoughts, feelings and behaviors. We strive to replace the old ways with healthier patterns of living.

Today the cycle of co-dependency stops with me. With the help of my Higher Power, I will not pass on to my family or friends the old thoughts, feelings and behaviors from which I am trying to release myself.

"Good for the body is the work of the body, and good for the soul is the work of the soul, and good for either is the work of the other."

Henry David Thoreau

The prognosis for our careers is not great if we are not feeling challenged or getting gratification in our jobs. When going into the office becomes drudgery and when there's nothing more to learn, it may be time for a change. But we may be unable to leave the position because we have become attached to the job for emotional security. As we think about our careers, we can evaluate where we are in relationship to them.

Today I must be happy with myself before I can be happy with my job. Today I will think about my work and my relationship to it.

"Every moment of your life is infinitely creative and the universe is endlessly bountiful. Just put forth a clear enough request, and everything your heart desires must come to you."

Shakti Gawain

There is a Power within us that can make all our dreams come true. Connecting with this inner Power brings peace, emotional and physical healing and serenity and, with the help of this Power, we can create the best life that we can envision. The same Power that governs the planets, the moon and the sun also flows through us. With a power this strong we can create the best life possible.

Today as I think quality thoughts, I create a quality life and I am living my life to its maximum potential.

"There is no more miserable human being than one in whom nothing is habitual but indecision."

William James

Life doesn't wait. How often do we let random events determine our fate? When fear or uncertainty prevent us from making decisions, our inaction makes them for us. Indecision is the worst decision of all because it makes us victims of life, not participants in it. Active decision-making is essential to our spiritual progress. We are co-participants in the outcomes of our lives as we actively make choices and pursue new ways with guidance from our Higher Power.

Today I take action where it is needed in my life. Once I make decisions to the best of my ability and do all that I can, I leave the rest to my Higher Power.

"Humility, that low, sweet root from which all heavenly virtues shoot."

Thomas Moore

What is humility? And what does it have to do with spiritual growth? Humility is facing the facts and owning up to them. It means being honest about who we have become. We put ourselves on the same plane with our fellow human beings by admitting that we have the same human shortcomings. Then we confess our need for a Power greater than ourselves to make our lives function and we humbly ask our Higher Power to remove our shortcomings and to guide us.

Today as I reflect on my life, I will accept the facts. Although I have come far, there is always further to go. I humbly ask forgiveness from those I have harmed and ask my Higher Power to remove my shortcomings.

"For me there is only the traveling on paths that have heart, on any path that may have heart. There I travel, and the only worthwhile challenge is to traverse its full length. And there I travel, looking, looking, breathlessly."

Carlos Castaneda

Some days we come to a fork in our road to spiritual healing. The road to the left takes us up the street of self-centeredness while the road to the right takes us up the lane of self-improvement. We stand at the fork and the choice is ours. Even when we feel down we can still take the uplifting path.

Today I am taking the scenic route. No matter how bad I feel inside I choose the road of optimism over despair.

"When you are making a success of something, it's not work. It's a way of life. You enjoy yourself because you are making your contribution to the world."

Andy Granatelli

Work addiction promotes an atmosphere of on-the-job unhappiness, instability and insecurity. Companies that breed work addiction have a work force that is less cohesive, less organized and more conflict-ridden. We can scrutinize our working environment for dysfunctional practices and detach ourselves from participating in these unhealthy interactions.

Today I look at what's going on around me at work. I detach myself from unhealthy situations and re-route my energies in a more positive direction.

"Our negative emotions are simply the result of an extensive pattern of scars and wounds that we have experienced."

Ken Keyes

It is impossible to reach adulthood and not have some battle scars from life. Obstacles and frustrations of everyday life provide us with material from which to grow spiritually. We are our own best healers of our wounded selves. If we remember that we are not controlled by our past, then with the help of our Higher Power we can change our old perceptions of the world and transcend our negative past.

Today I discard old thoughts and feelings that stand in the way of my personal growth. My future is filled with hope, happiness and optimism.

"Variety is the mother of Enjoyment."

Benjamin Disraeli

We sometimes unintentionally limit ourselves out of a need for security. The more choices we have in life, the scarier it can be. We can eliminate sameness from our lives by getting out of the rut in which we find ourselves. By doing this we eliminate boredom and roadblocks to personal growth. If we can choose one thing to do differently, no matter how small, that we have never done before, then we can stand back and watch ourselves grow.

Today I will examine my life and search for areas where I have limited my growth. I will eliminate sameness from my life and open myself to new experiences.

"You say you want 'to be somebody' — then apparently you don't want to be yourself."

Hugh Prather

The words we use reflect how we feel about ourselves. Songs we sing such as, "You're Nobody 'Til Somebody Loves You" tell us we need another human being to make us complete. The truth is that another person does not make us whole; we are already whole. We just need to know it and keep reminding ourselves of the fact.

Today I realize that I am somebody, just as I am. It is great being successful and prosperous and having another person with whom to share my life. But I do not need these worldly things to make me feel good about who I am. I already am a complete human being.

"You can't get to the fruit of the tree unless you go out on a limb."

Shirley MacLaine

Every day of recovery is risk taking. We take the risk of being betrayed every time we share our innermost feelings. We take the risk of being rejected every time we commit ourselves. We risk the unknown every time we pioneer into new areas of life.

Oh! But to live a life without sharing feelings, without loving, without exploring this wonderful world! It would hardly be a life worth living. Usually we find that the risks we take bring a fullness to our lives that we had never known before.

Today with the guidance of my Inner Power, I face life's challenges and risks. I do not settle for second best but live my life to the fullest.

"The higher the flame has leaped, the colder and deader the ashes."

Olive Schreiner

Lighting a candle at both ends makes it burn out more quickly and it's a fact of life that fast living causes fast burnout. When we devote too much time to our jobs for too long, we eventually burn out. Unfortunately, our burnout often affects family members as much as it does us. We can avoid burnout by making time for ourselves which provides us with healing opportunities for renewing the body, mind and spirit.

Today I take the necessary steps to prevent burnout before it occurs. I will pace my work and build into my day healing time for my sake as well as that of my family.

*"Who never doubted never half believed.
Where doubt there truth is — 'tis her shadow."*

Philip James Bailey

There will be days when self-doubt eats us alive but it is okay to doubt. Doubting is a natural part of the recovery process. It is okay to question our path rather than blindly accept what we hear because it is through doubt that truth is achieved. By giving ourselves permission to doubt and to work through it, our belief in the truth is stronger than ever.

Today I do not condemn myself for doubtful thoughts. I acknowledge them while resting assured that they too will pass. My belief and faith in a Universal Power is greater than any self-defeating images. I know that trust will return.

"Courage is to feel the daily daggers of relentless steel and keep on living."

Douglas Malloch

We look in the wrong place for courage. In *The Wizard Of Oz*, the cowardly lion looked everywhere for courage, except inside himself. Courage gives us spiritual strength to stand our ground to defend truth. It flows from our Higher Power and gives us the ability to change the things that are possible to change in our daily lives and to endure the things we cannot change.

Today and in times of great need I will look inside for the courage I need to endure any situation. I will draw my strength and fortitude from my Higher Power. That courage will get me through any obstacle I encounter during the day.

"God grant me the serenity to accept the things I cannot change, the courage to change the things I can, and the wisdom to know the difference."

Reinhold Niebuhr

We often feel compelled to complete certain tasks even when we don't want to do them. Nagging thoughts keep us restless and mentally preoccupied with the past and future. They prevent us from living our lives in the present. When we care about ourselves, we will put an end to this senseless mental torment.

Repeating The Serenity Prayer can help us slow down and see the truly remarkable things about ourselves and in our lives.

Today I will go with the flow of my Higher Power. When compulsions start to grip me, I will let my Universal Power manage them and will repeat The Serenity Prayer.

"The unexamined life is not worth living."

Plato

Why do we take on mountains of work, even when we know we're already overloaded? For us turning down work projects or cutting back on hours is like asking a heroin addict to refuse the next fix or the alcoholic to turn down the next drink. Busy orgies keep us separated from ourselves, but our value as human beings does not depend on how hard we push ourselves. Overloading subtracts from our value and prevents us from knowing and loving our human spirit.

Today I monitor my overloading habits. I will treat myself not as a workhorse but with the same dignity and respect I give to others.

"Were we to take as much pains to be what we ought, as we do to disguise what we are, we might appear like ourselves without being at the trouble of any disguise at all."

Francois de la Rochefoucauld

Sometimes we try to get through life by hiding from it. We keep our thoughts and feelings to ourselves and are afraid to let others know who we are. Keeping secrets maintains the sickness and prevents spiritual healing. Spiritual growth only comes through opening ourselves up and taking risks. We ask for forgiveness from our loved ones and friends. We look into our souls and around inside. Then we leave our shells where we tried to hide.

Today I open my mind to the boundless supply of the universe. I no longer have anything to hide.

"Wind moving through grass so that the grass quivers. This moves me with an emotion I don't even understand."

Katherine Mansfield

Our Higher Power is everywhere: in the trees, in the sunset, in the bird's twitterings, in the gurgles of a baby and in our emotions as we experience all these things. Our Higher Power is everywhere — outside and within ourselves. As we go about our day, let's remember that we are never alone. In times of great distress and great happiness, we are accompanied by the most loving and powerful force in the universe.

Today I will not speak but for once I will be spoken unto. I will listen, see, smell, taste and feel my Higher Power in everything that I do.

*"Emotions should be servants, not masters
— or at least not tyrants."*

Robert H. Benson

Many of us freeze emotions that we have not
fully experienced because we don't want to
feel them. These frozen feelings continue to
paralyze us in our current relationships. By
letting our emotions thaw and expressing them
as they de-ice, we can heal our inner selves. We
do it slowly and patiently with love for the ones
with whom we share the frozen feelings and, as
we grieve, we forgive all parties and we replace
the thawed feelings with love and understanding. Then happiness and joy find their way into
our lives.

*Today I make my emotions my servants
instead of my master. I thaw frozen feelings
and let the healing process begin.*

"Happiness is a function of accepting what is."

Werner Erhard

All of us want to be happy, but happiness often slips through our fingers. Happiness is not having what we want but wanting what we have. When we want what we already have, we express appreciation and gratitude for the fullness in our lives. When we want what we have, nothingness is transformed into abundance.

Today my happiness comes from within, not without. I do not depend on the outside world to make me happy. I do not need anything or anyone beyond what I already have to make me happy. I have everything I need for happiness to fill my life. Wanting what I have makes me happy and leaves me fulfilled.

"All work is as seed sown; it grows and spreads, and sows itself anew."

Thomas Carlyle

Those of us who are compulsive workers sometimes behave as if we have split personalities. Promises of spending time with our loved ones or of cutting down on work are broken. Our families learn that they cannot count on us. We become inconsistent and unpredictable. When we let worldly events guide us, our moods and behaviors are determined by everything and everyone but ourselves.

Today I will put my life on a steady course. My Higher Power is the barometer that keeps me centered. Stability and consistency are with me. I will only make promises that I can keep. I am dependable, responsible and trustworthy.

"Worry, the interest paid by those who borrow trouble."

George Washington Lyon

Asking ourselves "what if" questions is simply a way to generate needless anxiety and crisis in our lives. It is another form of negative thinking that expects the worst, therefore creating the worst that can happen. In recovery we do our best and accept the fact that "what ifs" are out of our control. We can take "what is" and leave "what ifs" for our Higher Power. Consequences and events are beyond our control but we can always think positive thoughts and trust our Higher Power.

Today I leave the actual workings of my life to a universe that is much more powerful than I am. I will take "what is" and leave the "what ifs" for my Higher Power.

"Never bear more than one kind of trouble at a time. Some people bear three kinds: all they have had, all they have now and all they expect to have."

Edward Everett Hale

Sometimes the hardest part of recovery for compulsive workers is when everything is going well. We are so accustomed to expecting only the worst that we do not know how to enjoy the best. These negative expectations do not serve us anymore. Our present mental attitudes determine what will happen and we can expect only the best.

Today all is well with me. As difficult times arise, I will use them as a chance to strengthen my faith in my Higher Power and my own spiritual growth. I choose peace and serenity in my life.

"Man does not simply exist, but always decides what his existence will be, what he will become in the next moment."

Viktor Frankl

During his three grim years of confinement at Auschwitz and other Nazi camps, Viktor Frankl was robbed of all human dignity. Still he always saw choices for himself and made them each day. His power of choice helped him survive the Holocaust.

No matter how difficult things seem, we *always* have choices. The event does not make decisions for us. We either let it make our choices or make our own independent of it.

Today I have the freedom to think and feel as I choose, no matter what happens in my life. I choose love, happiness and tranquility.

"I am only one, but still I am one. I cannot do everything, but still I can do something; and because I cannot do everything, I will not refuse to do something that I can do."

Edward Everett Hale

Our natural swing and style is to make sense out of the world we inhabit. All of us need a degree of self-control, but the greater the pressure, the more compulsively we seek control. We are unable to depend on others for help and we insist on doing everything ourselves. Giving up the need to control everything and admitting our powerlessness is the first step on our path of spiritual recovery.

Today I find peak performance in my life by giving up my obsessive urge to control. As I let go, order and tranquility fill my life.

"The world is not to be put in order, the world is order incarnate. It is for us to put ourselves in unison with this order."

Henry Miller

Freedom comes from knowing what our options are. Some things cannot be changed, no matter what. No matter how hard we try, we cannot make our world and the people in it behave as we want. It is not our responsibility to put the world in perfect order as we believe it should be. The world is perfectly ordered as it is. Our task is to stop trying to make trees fly and to put ourselves in unison with the universal flow.

Today I accept whatever comes my way. But in partnership with my Higher Power, I will decide what I think, how I feel and how I will respond.

" . . . *There is no better way to finish the spiritual life than to be ever beginning it over again, and never to think that you have done enough.*"

St. Francis de Sales

We can rediscover the world that we have lived in for so long and have taken for granted or ignored. We can look at people and places around us as if we are seeing them for the first time. We can take time out to smell the flowers. When we try this, we discover a world that we have never seen before.

Today I will use my senses to experience my world in a way that I have never experienced it before. I will stop to really see, taste, smell, feel and hear. As I do this, I discover that the little things that I have ignored are actually the most important things of all.

*"Every advance in spiritual life has its cor-
responding dangers; every step that we rise
nearer God increases the depth of the gulf into
which we may fall."*

Robert H. Benson

We are successful, accomplished and have
all of the material comforts of life. But why are
we so miserable and lonely inside? Those of us
who are co-dependent often feel that something is missing from our lives. The problem is
we suffer from spiritual bankruptcy because
we haven't put any effort into our spiritual
coffers. We substitute unhealthy relationships
for the spiritual hunger that only recovery can
satisfy.

*Today I am making daily deposits and my
spiritual life is growing steadily. I am richer
than ever before.*

"The greatest mistake you can make in this life is to be continually fearing you will make one."

Elbert Hubbard

One of the reasons we get stuck in accomplishing and achieving is that we are afraid of failure. We keep plugging away to produce so that no one will ever find out that we're not as great as everyone thinks. What we understand best are unhappiness and discontent and we accept them because they fit with our dysfunctional past. But the only way to prevent these feelings is to change our past thinking to healthier thoughts. As long as we fear failure, we will never know true success.

Today I welcome good things into my life. I deserve all the riches of the universe and accept them with open arms. As I experience success, I feel worthy and thankful.

"There is a great deal of self-will in the world, but very little genuine independence of character."

Frederick W. Faber

We sometimes need to detach ourselves from loved ones so that their problems do not divert us from our own spiritual path. The urge to fix others' lives, as our own crumble, interferes with our own spiritual development. Detachment without amputation allows us to remove ourselves from unhealthy situations out of love. We can love and help our fellow human beings only as much as we love and help ourselves.

Today I detach with love when appropriate. My Higher Power is the Great Controller, not me, and I will leave the management of the affairs of the universe up to this Power that can fix everything.

"The highest and most profitable reading is the true knowledge and consideration of ourselves."

Thomas à Kempis

It is important in our spiritual search that we take an honest inventory of ourselves. Identifying our strong and weak points helps us to see those traits that foster our growth and the growth of others and those that block spiritual growth. As we take personal stock, we refrain from putting ourselves down. We merely make an objective evaluation of dysfunctional thoughts and behaviors that have kept us from reaching our full potential.

Today I look at my life honestly by acknowledging my good points and my downfalls. I continue to love myself no matter what my inventory reveals.

"We are afraid to let go of our petty reality in order to grasp at a great shadow."

Antoine de Saint Exupéry

Remember the age-old question, "Is the hour-glass half empty or half full?" At 40 years of age, those of us who view our lives with despair think of life as half over but optimistic eyes view it as another exciting half to go. We make out of life what we want. We always have a choice in how we want to view our lives.

Today I choose to find exhilaration over misery, beauty over flaws and optimism over despair. I count my blessings and take whatever life brings me. And I will always look for the best in the worst.

"Man is born free, and everywhere he is in chains."

John Jacques Rousseau

Why do we feel like we are always putting out fires? Because we are always creating them. We can ask ourselves, "What do I gain from these crises?" Comfort? Success? Importance? Once we know, we can find more constructive ways of getting the same satisfaction knowing that inner satisfaction diminishes the need to derive it from the external world.

Today I will be aware of how easy it is to take an objective event and turn it into a crisis. I will ask myself what I gain from such behaviors. Whatever these gains are, I will get them met through healthy ways that bring no harm to myself or others.

"Many things which cannot be overcome when they are together, yield themselves up when taken little by little."

Plutarch

We cannot expect to change old thoughts and behaviors in one day, week or even a month. Recovery from co-dependency takes time, as does recovery from any addiction. When our personal growth is not moving fast enough for us, we need not become discouraged. We are on our Higher Power's schedule, not our own. Our spiritual recovery is already working when we admit we are powerless over the ability to control our lives.

Today I have hope and faith that I will eventually be where I want to be. But for now I will take it one baby step at a time.

"Seek not the depths of your knowledge with staff or sounding line, for self is a sea boundless and measureless."

Kahlil Gibran

Overachievers tend to be *quantitative* successes and *qualitative* failures. Often, we tend to feel like failures as human beings because we sacrifice the inward quality of life to outward success. Success in the material world does not automatically guarantee success of the human spirit. True success comes not just from human "doing," but from human "being."

Today as I strive to be successful in the world, I will not neglect my spiritual needs. If I fall in the corporate world, my spiritual success will always pick me up. I will seek balance in both worlds so that I can experience success in its totality.

"They talked about illness, money, shabby domestic cares. Their talk painted the walls of the dismal prison in which these men had locked themselves up."

Antoine de Saint Exupéry

We get stuck in a way of thinking and feeling that develops from growing up in dysfunctional families. But we are not prisoners of past experiences. Today we can transform all the negativity, self-doubt and self-defeat into more positive ways of thinking.

Today I am what I think of myself. I can change what I think of myself and thus, change my whole life. I am becoming more and more every day the kind of person I want to be. Today I am soaring in this spiritual transformation.

"Any man more right than his neighbors constitutes a majority of one."

Henry David Thoreau

Always being right is part of our dysfunction. No one is always right. Everybody makes mistakes now and then. Being right is what we want reality to be, not what it actually is, but admitting mistakes without self-condemnation and giving ourselves permission to be wrong are healthy signs in our spiritual growth. When we have self-confidence and inner security, admitting errors is not a threat to our self-esteem.

Today when I am wrong, I will admit it promptly, with self-forgiveness, as part of my human condition. I am learning that always being right is a burden that I no longer want or need.

"The more you learn to love and accept yourself, the more you will realize that you are doing exactly what you need to do to provide yourself with experiences to grow into higher consciousness."

Ken Keyes

Geographical escape doesn't help us find ourselves but so many of us on the fast track are so busy "getting there" that we forget we are already "there." There's nowhere to go. All we need to do is look within. We don't have to rush to get ahead because we already are ahead, when we know who we are.

Today I will be there with my life. In the swirl and confusion of the workday I have my Higher Power to remind me that there is really no place to go, because I am already there.

"Work of sight is done. Now do heart work on the pictures within you."

Rainer Maria Rilke

It can be lonely and frightening when others don't understand what it's like to be drowning in a sea of co-dependency. When we follow the lead of people-pleasing, guilt, "shoulds," busy schedules and solving the problems of others, our lives become totally unmanageable, but when we allow ourselves to be led from within, our lives tend to work. We learn that we can make good decisions and solve our own problems with the help of our inner guide.

Today I will not allow my self-will to lead me down the path of unhealthy relationships. My Higher Power is my leader and I will keep that inner focus and take my lead from within.

"Sin has many tools, but a lie is the handle which fits them all."

Oliver Wendell Holmes

For a lifetime we believe the lie: that we are stupid, unattractive and inferior; that the world is full of catastrophe, misery, poverty and suffering. We looked into the negative mirrors of those around us and learned to look at life and ourselves in the same destructive way. Spiritual healing is about reframing the mirrors we use in our spiritual search. We look back and examine the people who mirrored those destructive images to us and we see that things were not that way at all.

Today I will use the positive mirrors in my life as I continue my spiritual search. I will see my own human good and reflect the same to others in my life.

"Larceny is not a difficult crime to condone unless your childhood was the item stolen."

Pat Conroy

Our childhood feelings, thoughts and experiences are carried inside us throughout life. Buried deep within us the child cries out. Holding on to those old ways of being keeps us living in the past and we continue the immature thoughts and feelings that prevent us from developing to our fullest. Embracing and loving the buried child is healing. It helps us grow up, release old patterns and gain new, more mature ones.

Today I will reorganize my daily routines to bring out the buried child within me. I will know that I'm okay just as I am and I'm becoming better with each new day.

"Beggars do not envy millionaires, though of course they will envy other beggars who are more successful."

Bertrand Russell

How do we react when good things come to someone we know? Do we feel jealous or bitter? Coveting the good fortune of others is self-damaging and blocks our own spiritual growth, while rejoicing in the prosperity of others brings spiritual nourishment and good things flow from the universe.

Today I will rejoice in the good fortune of everyone I meet. I also give thanks for my own good fortune and pass these feelings on to others every chance I get.

"Don't push the river; it flows by itself."

Barry Stevens

Resistance in our daily lives thwarts the healing process and brings our recovery to a standstill. It stalls us on our spiritual path and complicates our lives. Surrender to resistance allows us to go with the flow and, rather than pushing against the current, to ride the river in the direction that it takes us. When we let go and let God, our lives flow with ease.

Today I do not allow resistance to stunt my growth. I will catch myself when I start to resist what life doles out. I open myself to the lessons that life teaches me and I do not fear the unknown because my Higher Power controls it.

"*When a man is wrapped up in himself, he makes a pretty small package.*"

John Ruskin

It's easy to get wrapped up in ourselves in recovery. We may spend so much time working on ourselves that we forget about the needs of others.

But self-centeredness is the other extreme of self-neglect. In recovery we seek to move to the middle of the line where our needs are met but not at the expense of others.

Through interacting with others we simply acquire more experience and strength to bring our lives into greater balance.

Today I take care of myself but do not become wrapped up in myself. I always have time to love and care for others.

"Indeed, it is not in human nature to deceive others for any long time, without in a measure deceiving ourselves too."

John Henry Newman

Sometimes we go to any length to practice our addictions, hiding the truth from loved ones. When our addictions are so strong that we are powerless over their pull, it's time to examine why by asking ourselves: Why does deception have such power and control over our lives?

Honesty frees us from self-deception. It teaches us to admit our wrongs and to forgive ourselves for them.

Today I take an honest look at my life and, with the help of my Higher Power, I remove deceit and right any wrongs that I find. I am becoming more honest and trustworthy with each new day.

"Toil, says the proverb, is the sire of fame."

Euripides

We can become emotionally paralyzed from life's problems. We feel powerless to do anything about them. So we just mope around hoping they will improve. Only self-action can change the negative course of our lives.

It is through life's painful challenges that we make our most significant gains. Spiritual growth is not effortless; we must do something to make it happen.

Today I will not let my life overpower me. When I am presented with difficult times, I will not sit and wait for things to correct themselves. I will take positive steps, through the Power that fills me up, to right the wrong and bring harmony back into my life.

"The lust for power is not rooted in strength but in weakness."

Erich Fromm

Sometimes we are deluded into thinking that acquiring power brings self-fulfillment. We are consumed by making it to the top.

Recovery teaches us that we are powerless by ourselves and our quest for power has made our lives unmanageable. But when we turn our will and our lives over to a Power greater than ourselves, we are ironically empowered.

Today I admit that I am powerless to manage my life. But a Power greater than me can restore it. Today I turn my will and my life over to the care of my Higher Power and receive abundance in life.

"The man who removed the mountain began by carrying away small stones."

Chinese Proverb

In the beginning spiritual growth is a new game. As with a child learning to play soccer, the skill comes gradually with practice and patience. So it is with healing ourselves.

The process of spiritual healing is like falling into a lake with rocks in our pockets. We sink to the bottom at first. But as we take one rock out at a time, we gradually rise higher and higher. Each day with practice we move up and grow in our understanding.

Today I practice spiritual healing in my life. I take it one rock at a time and my life unfolds with serenity and fulfillment.

"Human beings seem to have an almost unlimited capacity to deceive themselves, and to deceive themselves into taking their own lies for truth."

R. D. Laing

Switching from one addiction to another is a way of filling the inner void. But it is a masquerade in self-deception; we fool ourselves into believing that we have conquered our family dysfunction.

Switching to a spiritual path brings us true victory over family dysfunction and control of compulsive behaviors. It frees us from self-deception.

Today I will not fool myself into thinking that I have conquered my family dysfunction. I am powerless over my compulsions and know that my Higher Power can restore me to sanity.

"He who, from zone to zone, guides through the boundless sky thy certain flight, in the long way that I must tread alone, will lead my steps aright."

William Cullen Bryant

We are so accustomed to pleasing others and doing what is expected that we lose touch with the things we enjoy. We may no longer know what it is we want or need to do with our lives.

Beginning today, we can make a closer examination of our lives. Are we leading them? Or are they leading us? With the inspiration and support of our Higher Power, we can reclaim the lead in our lives rather than running a close second behind them.

Today I reclaim the lead in my life. Each day I ask for continued inspiration and guidance from my Higher Power.

"Trust is a treasured item and relationship. Once it is tarnished, it is hard to restore it to its original glow."

William A. Ward

When we trust, we put our hope and faith in our fellow human beings. Trust enables us to believe and rely on others while allowing them to do the same with us.

Fear is the greatest roadblock to trust. Trust in others and life itself follows once we begin to trust ourselves more and fear ourselves less.

Today I trust that the miraculous power of the universe responds to all of my needs. I have faith that my life is in good hands and that magnificent things are in store for me.

"Lost time is like a run in a stocking. It always got worse."

Ann Morrow Lindbergh

Time is a precious commodity. We do not like to be kept waiting in our fast-paced lifestyles. Hurried lifestyles leave no time for living within. Waiting, on the other hand, keeps us open and in constant contact with the spiritual flow. When we wait, we give up control and become receptive to life's blessings.

Today I give up the need to overstructure my life. I am learning to wait when I need to wait, knowing that I am receptive to the inspiration of inner guidance. Waiting will allow me to receive what I need to live a better life. Waiting brings me the strength to give.

"Restlessness and discontent are the first necessities of progress."

Thomas A. Edison

Why is it so hard for us to slow down and relax? Work is our sedative. It keeps us preoccupied from feelings and calms us down.

Restlessness is directly related to spiritual progress. When we are unsettled, we are at odds with ourselves. Our inner selves are unhappy, demanding attention. We're running on spiritual emptiness. Filling up this emptiness with spiritual fuel provides us with inner peace.

Today signs of restlessness tell me that I have neglected my spiritual needs. I will direct all thoughts to my inner self, an action that always restores my life to serenity.

"Your doubts are the private detectives employed by your dislikes, to make a case against change or choice."

W. R. Rodgers

As long as doubt precedes our path, we have no need for trust and faith because both require taking risks. We are constantly fleeing from uncertainty, change and choice. Doubt furnishes our dislikes with evidence to keep us from taking the risks needed for personal growth.

We can change the plot by employing trust and faith as our scouting party so that dislike, mistrust, fear and pessimism are cleared from our path.

Today I employ faith and trust as my private detectives to open up for me routes that help me grow and develop to my fullest.

"Healing is a matter of time, but it is sometimes also a matter of opportunity."

Hippocrates

The healing process is underway as we mend our ways, change our work habits, give up resistance in our lives and take more responsibility for our spiritual selves. We no longer resist change, discomfort or the unknown. As we stop resisting our life flow, we can feel the healing effects day by day, and we can see the consequences as they unfold in our daily lives. We still have problems and concerns, but we approach them in more optimistic and effective ways.

Today I am on the mend and my healing process is totally guided by my Higher Power who resides within me. I experience the healing effects in my interactions at home, at work and at play.

"Sometimes I want to write criticism a letter and tell him to leave me alone. The problem is that when I don't see him for a while, I start to miss him."

Ruth Gendler

Many of us feel more comfort and security living the life of an underdog than we do living on top. One of the greatest blessings of recovery is that we make peace with ourselves. Old thought patterns are replaced by healthier ones. We spend our days looking for beauty, peace, happiness and goodness.

Today I welcome all that is good in my life. I will notice the wonderful things around me, in others and in myself. I will radiate love and acceptance in all my daily transactions.

"Haste maketh waste."

John Heywood

When impatience leads to impulsiveness, nowhere is the adage "haste makes waste" more appropriate. Important decisions are made and projects launched before all facts are gathered, before all options are thoroughly explored or before all phases have been finalized. The results can be disastrous when our hurry sickness outruns careful thought and reflection. Waste not, want not. When we use our time wisely for balance in all areas of life, we lack for nothing.

Today I will make time for life's essentials — time for my loved ones and special time for me. Through these fruitful uses of my time, there can be no haste, waste or want.

"If you want to kill time, why not try working it to death."

O. A. Battista

The compulsion to work at the expense of all else is a sickness of the spirit, a loss of touch with what is important in life. It comes from a loss of meaning and purpose. This hurry sickness is attractive to us when we are not grounded in a strong spiritual base. Compulsive working gives us a false sense of security, power and control over our lives. In return it takes its toll. We die a slow painful death both spiritually and physically.

Today I am becoming more and more attracted to constructive pastimes in my life, not lethal ones. I am pulled to my Higher Power through its positive force. I am attracted to the joy of recovery and the fulfillment of life.

"The necessity of appearing in your own face. There are days when that is the last place in the world where you want to be but you have to be there, like a movie, because it features you."

Richard Brautigan

We are afraid that if someone leaves us, there will be nothing left but emptiness. We think we must have someone else to feel complete and worthy. These mistaken thoughts come from our dysfunctional pasts. We carry these empty feelings until we get in touch with our spiritual selves.

Once we start to know and value who we are and to love and care for ourselves, we feel complete just as we are and we never feel alone.

Today I am never alone as long as I have myself and my inner guide for company. Each day of my journey brings me closer to self-awareness, self-love and love of others.

"When love and skill work together, expect a masterpiece."

John Ruskin

Supervisors, peers or subordinates may carry family dysfunction into the workplace and recreate it in relationships with co-workers. Fear, insecurity and burnout are natural reactions in such unpredictable interactions on the job. When we must put up with such emotional battering, we end up limping through our careers.

When troubles befall us in our jobs, we can use them to become strong and confident. We can draw from our inner strength and fortitude and let our inner light shine through.

Today I use troubles on the job as experiences from which I can learn and grow. Tolerance, understanding and patience are my watchwords.

"Better to be a strong man with a weak point, than to be a weak man without a strong point. A diamond with a flaw is more valuable than a brick without a flaw."

William J.H. Boetcker

As we strive for excellence, it is important to expect and permit ourselves to make mistakes and to stop beating ourselves up when we do. Admitting the exact nature of our wrongs does not mean we become complacent or irresponsible. Admitting when we are wrong permits us to be human with all its imperfections. Like the diamond, it doesn't diminish our value; it makes us more valuable.

Today I will revise my perfectionistic standards into humanistic standards. I will build in margin for error and forgive myself and others for making mistakes as we strive to do the best we can.

"Part of self-acceptance is releasing other people's opinions."

Louise Hay

In childhood we internalize messages about ourselves that we get from adults. These messages — accurate or inaccurate — become our reality. In adulthood, the messages continue to remind us of who we are through mental chitchat. Inaccurate old chitchat damages our growth. Giving up these worn-out beliefs about ourselves and wiping the slate clean is the beginning of spiritual transformation.

Today is the first day of the remainder of my life. I am creating a new life in the present. That includes giving up the old dysfunctional life of the past. I ask my Higher Power to guide me in this spiritual transformation.

"Angels can fly because they take themselves lightly."

G. K. Chesterton

Some of us are moved to hysteria over the smallest things. When little things become overblown, it could mean we have lost perspective between significance and trivia.

Evaluating our lives and weighing our blessings with our burdens help us discover the truly important things. As we put our trials and tribulations in perspective, we realize that many of our trials are only trifles.

Today I will look for the abundance in my life. I will not let little things become burdensome. I will count my blessings and separate big concerns from small ones. I will approach my life with hope and optimism.

*"An appeaser is one who feeds a crocodile —
hoping it will eat him last."*

Winston Churchill

Why is it so important to us what others
think? Pleasing others comes from not knowing
and appreciating who we are. When we try to
please, our personalities change with the wind.
We lose our self-respect and others lose respect
for us. The adage "To thine own self be true" is
simple but wise. A strong spiritual connection
gives us the foundation to stand firm on who
we are and what we believe in. We please
ourselves first and do not waver under pressure
from others.

*Today I will live my life according to what
is right for me. I will not judge what others
do and I will not let their judgments sway
me from my spiritual path.*

"The quieter you become, the more you can hear."

Ram Dass

Prayer is one of the major tools of recovery. There is always time for prayer and it can happen anywhere: in a traffic jam or in private. Prayer can be silent meditation where all thoughts are voided. It can be silently waiting for new answers to come or an expression of humility when asking for daily strength and guidance from a Greater Power.

Prayer serves as a lifeline to a spiritual way of life and connects us to our Higher Power. It takes us from the darkness of despair to the light of self-fulfillment.

Today prayer is a part of my spiritual program. I will pray when waiting, before sleeping and when inspired. My prayers are always answered and keep me centered and content.

"When we desire to encourage the growth of the human spirit, we challenge and encourage the human capacity to solve problems, just as in school we deliberately set problems for our children to solve. It is through the pain of confronting and resolving problems that we learn."

M. Scott Peck

Overcoming barriers promotes personal growth as we learn from each experience and grow in spiritual strength.

Without obstacles to work through, life would be dull indeed. There would be no reason to live. We would be without challenge, without purpose.

Today as I encounter obstacles in life, I will not run or resist. Facing experiences with divine guidance from my Higher Power, I will learn and grow from them.

"Much more happiness is to be found in the world than gloomy eyes discover."

Friedrich Wilhelm Nietzsche

Murphy's Law says, "Whatever can go wrong, will go wrong." When we live by this law, we expect the worst life has to offer. The likelihood is that the worst will happen. When negative thoughts haunt our minds, we create self-defeating lives for ourselves.

The words we use reveal how the old negative thoughts dominate our lives through our actions. Rephrasing negative thoughts into positive ones (such as "Good luck follows me everywhere I go") can start a healthier and happier way of being.

Today impending doom is only a thought I can erase from my mind. My life is no longer dictated by the negative and I am creating a world of impending optimism.

"The way to do is to be."

Lao Tzu

Fast-track living and compulsive working turn us into human doers, not human beings. We live in the past and future rather than the present. It is difficult for us to relax, do nothing and enjoy the now. Idle time makes us anxious and worthless because we are unproductive. The compulsion to *do* always seems to overpower the desire to *be*.

Through spiritual growth, we move from human *doing* to human *being*. Our self-worth is no longer dominated by work. As we let ourselves be, we start to become, one day at a time, all that we are capable of being.

Today I give myself permission to be. Yesterday I was, tomorrow I will be and today I am.

"The more I give myself permission to live in the moment and enjoy it without feeling guilty or judgmental about any other time, the better I feel about the quality of my work."

Wayne Dyer

Fast-trackers spend a lot of time mentally planning and thinking about future events. We have repeated episodes of brownouts or forgetfulness because of burnout and because our minds are concentrating on completing the next task, rather than the present moment.

By living our lives in the present, we experience the spontaneity and beauty that fill our day from moment to moment.

Today I live my life in the now. I concentrate on the truly important things around me from second to second.

"No pleasure is comparable to the standing upon the vantage ground of truth."

Francis Bacon

New doors are never opened without the desire for truth. There is a Power greater than ourselves, and this Power can restore us to sanity. This truth is always within us but stubborn self-will continues to dodge it. We think we can control our own lives.

Dodging the truth keeps us from growing and coping from day to day. Facing the truth comes with opening our hearts to the healing might of our Higher Power.

Today I ask myself if I am dodging the truth. As truth comes to me, I will not dodge it. I will let the truth of my Higher Power shine through my thinking and doing always.

"The child inside you wants to be impulsive and adventuresome, without always having to plan things in advance."

Wayne Dyer

Routines and schedules. We need them in today's busy world to keep our lives orderly. We can ask ourselves: How many wonderful experiences and people do we exclude by living our lives by the book?

Many times we lead our lives in rigid step-by-step fashion because it gives us control, security and predictability. When we turn our lives over to our Higher Power, we flow with the plot that life writes for us daily. Doing just one thing in a daily routine differently can break the monotony of living by the book.

Today I will save some time to experience what life has in store for me. I will look for spontaneity and flexibility in my daily interactions.

"In the circles where self-contempt is preached, it is of course never explained why a person should be so ill-mannered and inconsiderate as to force his company on other people if he finds it so dreary and deadening himself."

Rollo May

As long as we think of ourselves as worthless or inferior, we will never be successful in life. Once we get out of our own way by renouncing negative feelings, we remove the major roadblock on our spiritual path. We can step aside, let go and self-fulfillment is ours.

Today I will release all of my self-debasing thoughts and feelings. I am the only problem standing in the way of my happiness. I will step aside and let my Higher Power show me the way.

"Love does not consist in gazing at each other but in looking outward together in the same direction."

Antoine de Saint Exupéry

Co-dependency with another person or a job prevents personal growth. We can think of ourselves and our spouses as giant trees with branches intertwined and leaning on each other for support.

Recovery teaches us that we are separate giant trees that grow straight and tall, not leaning on another tree for survival. Our branches may touch the giant oak beside us, but we grow strong and independent of it.

Today I become my own person and stand firm like a giant oak. I will make decisions about my thoughts and feelings, regardless of the moods of loved ones and situations.

*Searching — earnestly and secretly — the
   sacred quest,
Engulfs our being and carries us,
Lowering us deeply to the core of our essence,
Faltering as we question, affirm and love what
   we discover!*

Bryan Robinson

So many of us are searching for meaning in
our empty lives. We search high and low, far
and wide. We ask our therapists; we read
books; we jump into the latest "growth craze"
for the answers. We make this search so complicated, when it is really so simple. What we
are looking for is right under our eyes: our true
inner selves.

*Today I ask for divine guidance as I go
within to find the meaning in my life. I will
get in touch with my Higher Self which fills
that inner void.*

"The diamond cannot be polished without friction, nor the man perfected without trials."

Chinese Proverb

Relapses occur when chronic overachieving and the needs of others take precedence over everything else in our lives. We feel vulnerable, scared, dependent, isolated and victimized.

We can slow down and think things through before making commitments and say "no" more often. Ultimately, meeting the demands of our inner needs brings us inner peace and harmony. Relapse is one of the few guarantees that we get with recovery.

Today when I feel myself moving backward, I let go and let God. My Higher Power turns me around and points me in the direction I need to move. All is right in my world.

" . . . *I neglect God and his angels, for the noise of a fly, for the rattling of a coach, for the whining of a door.*"

John Donne

When we try to squeeze more work into less time, eventual burnout is the consequence. When fatigue and stress escalate, the likelihood of accidents and errors also increases. Continual overinvestment in jobs results in burnout and the decline of work efficiency.

All of us who live in the fast lane need refueling time. Hobbies, exercise, creative pursuits and social pastimes are ways of refueling.

Today is refueling day. I will set aside a time to collect my thoughts and do something special for myself. As I do one enjoyable thing I haven't done in a long time, I feel my life refueling and expanding.

"Be like a bird, halting in his flight a while in boughs so light, feels them give way beneath him and yet sings, knowing that he hath wings."

Victor Hugo

Belief in a Power greater than us is sustaining. When self-will drags us down, our Higher Power lifts us up.

Our Higher Power is ever present. That's why we no longer have to worry when we turn our life and will over to a Power greater than ourselves. We know that everything that happens does so for a reason, although we don't always know what the reason is.

Today I will use my spiritual foundation as a remedy to life's problems. As I yield to my Higher Power, I achieve soundness of body, mind and spirit and soar to unknown heights.

"What we call reality is an agreement that people have arrived at to make life more livable."

Louise Nevelson

Is it possible that we spend so much time working on our spiritual development that we get into the same position from which we are trying to escape? We can transfer our codependency into the spiritual realm and become spiritual junkies. Without daily interactions in the physical world, there can be no spiritual growth. The key to recovery resides in the balance of mind, body and spirit.

Today I am balancing going within and without. I know that to develop spiritually, I must keep constant contact with the physical world. I view each of my interactions as chances to practice new and healthier ways of thinking and behaving.

"It is Faith who protects Doubt from Cynicism."

Ruth Gendler

In recovery we don't try to figure everything out. An overdependence on logic and reason can restrain our spiritual growth. Faith replaces them as the tools of the spiritual domain which is beyond human touch. Recovery is based on faith, without observable proof. The more we believe in a spiritual growth, the more we change and the stronger our faith. It's something we believe in, feel and live.

Today self-doubt and lack of faith will not divert me from my course. I do not look for proof in the outside world. I already have all the evidence I need from changes in the way I feel inside.

"Until we lose ourselves, there is no hope of finding ourselves."

Henry Miller

A pitfall of recovery is that we can spend so much time immersed in our own egos that we become self-centered. We lose empathy and compassion for others and we forget that there are other viewpoints.

A large part of healing is getting our minds off our egos and being able to show compassion for others. Understanding how they feel from their point of view teaches us to let go of our rigid perceptions and to be more sensitive to the needs of others.

Today putting myself in someone else's place and showing compassion will further enrich my own life. I will take another point of view and practice compassion and understanding with that person.

"Let everyone sweep in front of his own door and the whole world will be clean."

Johann von Goethe

Many of us are super-responsible when it comes to getting the job done at work. But when it comes to taking an active role in family life, we often shirk our responsibilities. We are too busy to spend quality time with our loved ones. We are also irresponsible when it comes to keeping ourselves physically and mentally healthy. Our spiritual development goes down the tubes.

Recovery shows us the middle ground in our lives. And we learn to spend fewer waking hours being super-responsible workers and more time playing and living our lives.

Today I am not super-human, but I am a responsible person. I will spread responsibility throughout my life, not confine it to just one part.

"Coming together is a beginning; keeping together is progress; working together is success."

Jacob Braude

Creative solutions to many problems come from a team approach that generates many possibilities. Too few of us are team players. We believe our approach and style are the best answers and cannot entertain less perfect ideas.

We ask our Higher Power to release us from the need to be in charge. This releases us from our rigid mindsets and opens us to the spontaneous and creative flow of the universe.

Today I let my Higher Power be in charge of my life at work, at home and at play. As I live under this greater direction, my life runs like a smooth and soothing brook. Tranquility is restored.

"Grant that I might not criticize my neighbor until I have walked a mile in his moccasins."

Louise Garfield Munroe

Every time we condemn or make fun of someone else, we injure ourselves. All the negative energy we put out returns to smack us in the face. When we make other people the target of our discord, we often project our own faults onto them. It is time to look within at our own spiritual progress.

Today every time I have the urge to malign someone, I will stop and ask myself if I am without fault. I will put my energy into getting my own affairs in order. Looking for the good and beauty in others will help me see the good and beauty in myself.

"Man's many desires are like the small metal coins he carries about in his pockets. The more he has, the more they weigh him down."

                                        Satya Sai Baba

When we succumb to temptation, we operate from old patterns. But in resisting temptation we employ new ways of living that we have learned in our spiritual quest. The true test of success, however, is forgiving ourselves when we yield to whatever tempts us. Temptations are strategically placed on the road of recovery. We can never eliminate them, but we can eliminate unhealthy responses to them.

Today I am aware of my powerlessness. I will face temptations one by one and use the lessons they teach me in my spiritual growth.

"The inner side of every cloud is bright and shining; I therefore turn my clouds about, and always wear them inside out, to show the lining."

Ellen T. Fowler

Growing up in dysfunctional families where rejection, abuse and neglect are common leaves emotional wounds. We cannot change what happened to us, but we can heal our feelings about it.

Healing these wounds takes a recovery program that helps us disavow these attitudes and change them to more positive beliefs about ourselves.

Today my wounds from the past are healing more and more. I am separating the clouds of the past and uncovering the real hidden beauty in myself as each day unfolds.

"Work, and thou wilt bless the day ere the toil be done; they that work not, cannot pray, cannot feel the sun."

John Sullivan Dwight

In recovery every day is labor day because we are constantly working on ourselves. Spiritual development does not result from sitting back and waiting for a Higher Power to do everything for us. It takes effort on our part. There is never a time when we can rest on our laurels, for that is when relapse tries to re-enter our lives. Every day is a labor of love.

Today I will set aside time to work on my spiritual growth. When I start to feel discouraged, I will remember that things of value don't come easy. That's what makes them valuable.

"It is not wisdom to be only wise, and on the inward vision close the eyes."

George Santayana

Wisdom is something we rarely seek directly. It is a bonus gift that comes with spiritual progress.

How often do we waste our energies fighting things that are not worth our time and that we cannot change anyway? When disturbing events arise, we can ask ourselves if there is anything about the situation we can change. Once we learn to distinguish between the changeable and unchangeable, we achieve a high level of serenity and inner peace. This is the gift of wisdom.

Today I ask that God grant me the serenity to accept the things I cannot change, courage to change the things I can and wisdom to know the difference.

"He drew a circle that shut me out — Heretic, rebel, a thing to flout. But Love and I had the wit to win: We drew a circle that took him in!"

Edwin Markham

Carrying resentments and animosities eats away at us like a disease. It clouds our perceptions of situations and other people. It keeps our thinking distorted and our thoughts always focused on the negative. It weighs us down. Spiritual progress takes that weight off our shoulders. We feel cleansed and renewed. Having released the old, we are now ready to receive the new.

Today I will inventory my feelings for old grudges and where they exist, I will let them go. As I give them up, I feel healed and further along the road of recovery. I am a happier and healthier person as a result.

"I think, therefore I am."

Descartes

Without thinking, there could be no recovery. Our ability to think helps us make choices and decisions in our daily lives. Thinking endows us with the ability to act instead of react. Thinking helps us in our spiritual reflection and prayer. It helps us to understand how we can release old patterns and change for the better.

On our own we don't always make the best choices and decisions. But when we remember we have a Higher Power and many tools of recovery, we can create a happy and satisfying life for ourselves. We do not impose our realities on anyone else, nor do we allow theirs to be imposed upon us.

Today I think; therefore I am recovering.

"*I expect to pass this way but once; any good therefore that I can do, or any kindness that I can show to any fellow creature, let me do it now.*"

Etienne de Grellet

All of us are prophets, bearing messages for one another. It is through one another that our Higher Power speaks to us and works through us to help others. The Power also works through others to help us. Unexpected events and conversations often reveal solutions and answers when we are faced with problems. The goal of recovery is not spiritual perfection, but spiritual progress.

Today I will open my eyes and ears to get the messages I need from people and events in my daily life. I will be aware that what I say and do can affect the lives of others in more ways than I may realize.

"Fear has a large shadow, but he himself is quite small."

Ruth Gendler

One of the first steps in conquering fear is to identify what the fear is. Identifying the fear diffuses it, and it loses some of the power to dominate us. We realize that we have nothing to fear but fear itself. Fears are only thoughts and feelings we have created that may never come to pass.

The only way to conquer fear is to give it up. Letting our Higher Power take charge and saying The Serenity Prayer brings tranquility and puts all outcomes in the hands of a force that can make a difference.

Today when fear overtakes me, I will identify what it is and put it in the hands of my Higher Power. Once I let go and let God, miracles happen.

*"The finer the nature, the more flaws it will
show through the clearness of it; and it is a law
of this universe that the best things shall seldom-
est be seen in their best form."*

John Ruskin

Being willing means agreeing to give up a
way of life that hasn't worked anyway. We are
prepared to relinquish the need to control, to
be perfect, to be on top and the compulsion to
spend our time rushing and doing instead of
listening and watching. Being willing means
opening ourselves up to the unknown and the
unexpected, to a new way of life with all its
possibilities of change.

*Today I am willing to have all my short-
comings removed. I am ready to trade in my
old life for a new, more healthy one.*

"There are nettles everywhere. But smooth green grasses are more common still; the blue of heaven is larger than the cloud."

Elizabeth Barrett Browning

Sometimes it takes a jolt for us to realize how truly fortunate we are. The day-to-day annoyances we complain about are suddenly trivial when we face a major catastrophe. We gripe and complain about minor inconveniences when our lives are already rich and full. We can count our blessings, be thankful for all that we have and save complaining for the rare and important obstacles in life.

Today I will not let pettiness distract me from the more important things in life. I count my blessings for all that I have on this day.

"Within you there is a stillness and sanctuary to which you can retreat at anytime and be yourself."

Hermann Hesse

Our daily lives are super-charged and we are still on fast-forward after hours. We don't know how to cut ourselves off from work long enough to unwind. The first rule of thumb is to provide ourselves a mental sanctuary where neither thoughts of work nor items representing it are present. We can create this inner place of calm, harmony and contentment anywhere and anytime we can find stillness. There we will find answers to our worldly troubles.

Today I will build breathers into my work day. I can always go to my inner sanctuary to become refreshed, relaxed and recharged and find solutions to life's problems.

"Know thyself."

Socrates

Knowing who we are is the key to spiritual growth. We must first know and understand ourselves. We must love ourselves first and foremost and love of others will follow.

Because we are always changing and in the process of becoming, we never arrive at a point when we truly know who we are. We must get reacquainted with ourselves on a daily basis. Thus, recovery is a never-ending process requiring ongoing self-reflection and self-affirmation. As we work through our daily problems, we rediscover ourselves constantly.

Today as I examine the person I have become, I find a new friend and feel self-renewed. I keep myself open to rediscovering myself day by day.

"Work is the refuge of people who have nothing better to do."

Oscar Wilde

For some of us, jobs, the company and workplace are the central focus of our lives. Everything else — family, social life and self — revolves around them, like planets around the sun. Work organizations, like addictions, can never replace or satisfy the needs of family, friends and self.

We can look at the orbit of our lives and ask ourselves what's in the center and what we revolve around. We can make work one of our satellites, along with the other important stars in our lives.

Today I will ponder over my dependency on work to fulfill all my needs. I am drawn to the other satellites in my life on an equal basis.

"She will show us her shoulder, her bosom, her face; but what the heart's like, we must guess."

Edward Robert Bulwer Lytton

Without truthfulness to ourselves and others, there can be no spiritual progress. We must be truthful about our feelings as well as about the things that happen in our daily lives. We have become so accustomed to rearranging the truth in our lives that some of us believe the falsehoods that we tell. Being honest with ourselves keeps us consistent in what we say and do and lets others know we can be loved and trusted.

Today I will take a truthful look at how I conduct my business and personal affairs. I will replace half-truths, lies and dishonesty with the truth as it is shown to me.

"Happy the man who has broken the chains which hurt the mind, and has given up worrying once and for all."

Ovid

Worrying is just another habit of trying to control our destinies. If there's nothing in our own lives to fret about, then we create something. It is not our duty to bear the weight of the world. By getting rid of compulsive worry, we free ourselves to concentrate on the areas where we can make a difference. No longer distracted, we are clear of mind and purpose.

Today I take the concerns in my life I usually worry about, no matter how big or small, and put them in my Higher Power's hands. I put my energy to use on things in my life that I can change and I make those changes as my day unfolds.

"When Nature her great masterpiece de-sign'd, and fram'd her last best work, the hu-man mind, Her eye intent on all the wondrous plan, She form'd of various stuff the various Man."

Robert Burns

Thank goodness for individuality! If every-body thought alike, we would live in a mentally and emotionally impoverished world. Nothing would change. We would become rigid, boring and stuck on our spiritual journey.

Today I welcome opposing views, knowing that everyone's way of thinking is different from mine but valid nonetheless. I can seize viewpoints that challenge mine as an opened door to new ways of thinking and being.

*"My crown is in my heart, not on my head;
not deck'd with diamonds and Indian stones,
nor to be seen: my crown is called content; a
crown it is that seldom kings enjoy."*

William Shakespeare

A need for omnipotence, to have everything our way, stems from deep-seated feelings of discontent, insecurity and low self-worth. We have not admitted our powerlessness and surrendered to a Higher Power. Self-contentment is ours when we see that we are powerless over other people and events. We give up trying to force things to our views, negotiate and compromise in our daily interactions and live with equality rather than superiority.

Today I wear the crown of contentment. I am not the ruler of others; I can only control my thoughts and actions to the best of my ability.

"I saw that nothing was permanent. You don't want to possess anything that is dear to you because you might lose it."

Yoko Ono

We fear abandonment because we felt abandoned emotionally or physically earlier in our lives and the fear lives on in our minds.

Once we believe and accept a Higher Power, we are never alone in this relationship. We come to see that we created this false belief ourselves. Fear of abandonment melts away as we find our spiritual selves. Inner peace comes through being, not possessing.

Today I will be my own person, cooperative and kind, but genuinely me. I will think, feel and do what feels right and healthy. I have myself and my Higher Power is my sidekick. I vow to never abandon myself again.

"A mind all logic is like a knife all blade. It makes the hand bleed that uses it."

Rabindranath Tagore

The purpose of spiritual life is to synchronize ourselves with the universal scheme. Connecting with our spiritual selves puts us in touch with our Higher Power and the flow of the universal mainstream.

We cannot live in this flow 24 hours a day because we live in a physical world. We move in and out of it as we grow. Balancing our spiritual and physical realities leads to deep appreciation and fulfillment.

Today I am connected to the universal mainstream which sustains me through life's daily challenges. I draw from this spiritual connection to keep myself centered in all my worldly affairs.

"He that lacks time to mourn, lacks time to mend."

Sir Henry Taylor

Grieving is feeling the inner hurt and pain fully so that it will melt away. It is healing and healthy to grieve. Grieving includes crying out our feelings, pounding them out on a pillow, sharing them with a friend or counselor, writing them out on paper or talking them into a tape recorder. We are never alone in our grief because it is universal. When we share our grief, it becomes only half a grief.

Today when I feel a sense of loss, I will not withhold it. I will grieve it because I know grief soothes and heals my inner self. If someone else grieves, I will be there for them, for I know my presence will cut their pain in half.

"If a man has nothing to eat, fasting is the most intelligent thing he can do."

Hermann Hesse

We live on a planet that is perfectly planned. We try to alter the universal laws to fit what we want. As long as we conduct our lives without guidance from a universal Knowing, we will make a mess of things because we still don't know the rules. Once we learn the rules by which the universe operates, we fit into the grand harmony. Peace, happiness and tranquility are ours.

Today I practice hands off and follow the grand harmony of my Higher Power. I am learning the rules of life and how fitting into them can foster my spiritual growth.

"True contentment depends not upon what we have; a tub was large enough for Diogenes, but a world was too little for Alexander."

Charles Caleb Colton

Some of us have thought of ourselves as failures for a lifetime. We tell ourselves that nothing we ever do is good enough. The flaws always stand out.

As long as we are stuck in defeat, we will experience defeat. When we are ready and willing to accept our success as success and not as defeat, we will become successful.

Today I will credit myself with my successes, no matter how small. Even in defeat I taste success because there is nothing wrong with me. Life is simply teaching me how to be successful and to think successfully.

"There is a glory in a great mistake."

Nathalia Crane

When we admit to God, to ourselves and to another human being our wrongs, we are well into recovery. It means giving up our rationalizations, justifications and alibis for our shortcomings. It means being honest with ourselves. It means acknowledging our past self-righteous behaviors without guilt or self-condemnation. When we admit we are wrong, we make giant strides in developing our integrity and genuineness as a human being. And we commit ourselves to future spiritual growth.

Today when I am wrong, I will promptly admit it rather than engage in deception and rationalization. I commit myself to changing past wrongdoings in my future personal growth.

"Little strokes, fell great oaks."

Benjamin Franklin

A couple arrived in England on their way to visit relatives in Scotland and discovered the country had come to a transportation standstill because of a national rail strike. There were no trains, rental cars, buses or boat tickets. Their only recourse was to hitchhike along the motorway, which they did with some fear and hesitancy. The experience turned out to be the best vacation of their lives. They met interesting people, learned about the politics and customs firsthand and got to see more of the countryside than they would have by train.

Today I will persist in the face of opposition. I will persist with many different approaches to life's challenges until a path is cleared for me.

"It ain't no use to grumble and complain, it's just as cheap and easy to rejoice; When God sorts out the weather and sends rain, w'y rain's my choice."

James Whitcomb Riley

When something happens to us, it is not the situation that upsets us, but the way we think and feel about it. The event or action is not good or bad; it just *is*. The minute we judge it based on our subjective thoughts, we are emotionally involved in it. Negative thoughts keep us isolated from our spiritual selves. But when we expect the best, our lives are filled with abundance and joy.

Today I will expect the best life has to offer. I will look for the good in myself and in others and welcome the positive returns on my mental outlook.

"A really busy person never knows how much he weighs."

Edgar Watson Howe

We've seen them before: Motorists reading the newspaper, talking on the telephone or eating lunch as they speed to get somewhere. When behind the wheel of a car, our compulsive working can be as deadly as an alcoholic stupor. We suffer from the same lack of sobriety as the alcoholic.

We achieve work sobriety when we admit that our lives have become unmanageable and we drive under the influence of our Higher Power. Our values are restored and our thinking cleared.

Today I think about how I am managing my life. I ask my Higher Power to restore clarity and work sobriety to my life.

"Monotony is the law of nature. Look at the monotonous manner in which the sun rises. The monotony of necessary occupations is exhilarating and life-giving."

Mahatma Gandhi

It is easy to get bored with the everyday humdrum of our lives. The excitement and wonder are gone. We've done it all. Life is not stimulating anymore. Is that all there is?

When we are engaged in spiritual search, we are on a perpetual treasure hunt. We discover new and exciting things about ourselves. We unravel the mystery that surrounds our lives.

Today I look at the ordinary and the usual in a different way. I look behind them to see what treasures lurk there.

"He trudg'd along unknowing what he sought, and whistled as he went, for want of thought."

John Dryden

Balancing our work schedules with family, social and spiritual lives is a tightrope act. We never achieve perfect balance in anything, but we can strive to keep our lives well rounded. With a little thought and practice we develop the skills necessary for balance. As we reorganize our lives to allow more space for spiritual growth, family and social pastimes, our jobs become proportionate to these other life commitments. We approach balance in our daily affairs and live our lives to the fullest.

Today I strive for a well-rounded life, not a perfect one. As I strive for balance within myself, at home, at work and at play, I live my life to my fullest potential.

"The greatest of faults, I should say, is to be conscious of none."

Thomas Carlyle

How often do we try to blame other people for our own shortcomings? How many times have we unleashed our hostility and frustrations on innocent bystanders? When things don't go the way we want, we can first look within ourselves for the reasons. We can ask ourselves how we have created the problems we face and how we can resolve them responsibly without finding a scapegoat. Facing the outcomes of our own actions takes us from spiritual adolescence to spiritual maturity.

Today I face the consequences of my own behaviors with no scapegoats to blame. I admit the mistakes I make and do my best to right my wrongdoings.

"Be not forgetful of prayer. Every time you pray, if your prayer is sincere, there will be new feeling and new meaning in it, which will give you fresh courage, and you will understand that prayer is an education."

Fyodor Dostoyevsky

In recovery, conscious contact means making connections with a universal Power. Seeking conscious contact enables us to know our Higher Power better. We keep in contact through meditation and prayer for knowledge of our Higher Power's will for us and the power to carry that out.

Today my daily meditations and prayers keep me consciously connected with the Greater Power of the universe. I let go of my cares and let the will of my Higher Power be done.

"Birds of a feather flock together."

Miguel de Cervantes

We unconsciously surround ourselves with people with whom we feel comfortable and familiar. When we are troubled and confused, we are attracted to troubled and disturbed personalities. The company we keep rubs off on us, and we on them. We influence each other's thoughts and behaviors through a reciprocal cycle of interactions.

We can break this cycle by evaluating the company we keep. We seek out relationships with people who mirror and affirm our true value.

Today I take stock of the company I keep. I surround myself with people who help me grow and fulfill my potential.

"Be ashamed to die until you have won some victory for humanity."

Horace Mann

Nothing can ever be lost through spiritual giving. When we give freely and unselfishly without expecting anything in return, we always receive abundance from the universe. This practice is not motivated by guilt, neediness or dependence. Instead, it reflects our spiritual awakening. As we help others transform their lives, we are simultaneously and spiritually strengthened by our experiences.

Today I practice all the spiritual love and good that I can. I give freely and unselfishly and, where appropriate, anonymously to those in need.

"Step softly, under snow or rain, to find the place where men can pray; the way is all so very plain that we may lose the way."

G. K. Chesterton

What addictions do we use to hold our spirits up and to keep us going? Other people? Alcohol? Food? Work? Worrying? Sex? We are spiritually disabled as long as we are co-dependent.

In recovery we throw down our addictive crutches and walk on our own with spiritual strength from our Higher Power, a strength that sustains us no matter how difficult the pace. We trade in the crutches for something far more substantial — a greater understanding of the universe, ourselves and our relationship to life.

Today I discard the addictive crutches I've used to live my life. I walk on my own down the spiritual road with the full support of my Higher Power.

"The first and worst of all frauds is to cheat oneself."

Philip James Bailey

Self-deception is the refusal to see things as they truly are. It causes us to deny ourselves the same kindness and self-respect we give to and expect from others.

Self-insight helps us see ourselves as we really are. It helps us take an honest inventory of deceptive thoughts and behaviors that have held us back. The sunlight of self-insight lifts the fog of self-deception from our spiritual lives.

Today I let go of self-deception and see myself as I really am. I refrain from putting myself down in any way and accord myself the same respect as I would any other human being.

"Sunshine is delicious, rain is refreshing, wind braces us up, snow is exhilarating; there is really no such thing as bad weather, only different kinds of good weather."

John Ruskin

There are those days we dread facing. We don't want to get out of bed because we fear the unknown or it may be raining. We start with putting one foot in front of the other. We look for one thing in the day, no matter how small, that will bring a tinge of excitement. We compliment one person, smile at another and look for something extraordinary. By the end of the day dread turns into delight.

Today I have plenty of time to do all that needs to be done. Between the hours of nine and five I have the company of my inner self and know all will work satisfactorily.

"Walk on a rainbow trail; walk on a trail of song, and all about you will be beauty. There is a way out of every dark mist, over a rainbow trail."

Navajo Song

We are not always aware that we go about our days collecting evidence of our self-worth like butterflies in a net. At the end of the day we sort and classify our collection of negative comments, defeats and mistakes. Had we aimed our net in another direction, we would have a collection of compliments, successes and joys. We can ask ourselves what kinds of evidence about ourselves we collect.

Today my inner guide helps me look for the exceptional part of me that will add to my new collection of my self-worth.

"Procrastination is the art of keeping up with yesterday."

Don Marquis

Putting things off can eat away at us. Procrastination can make us anxious, irritable and even cause us to dislike ourselves. Our long lists and daily piles of chores weigh us down and clog our spiritual path. Just choosing one item from the list and completing it lifts the burden of procrastination. We start to feel less defeated and more hopeful about our day. We can do whatever needs doing one at a time and not worry about the mountain of nonessentials.

Today I don't let procrastination get the best of me. I distinguish between essentials and nonessentials and work through the things that must be done one at a time within my human limitations.

"No one can develop freely in this world and find a full life without feeling understood by at least one person."

Paul Tournier

Many times we feel we are the first to go through a particular experience. We think our feelings are unique to us and that no one else could possibly understand them. But in our daily readings and talks with others who do understand, we discover that we are not alone with our experiences or feelings. Understanding the pain of someone else helps minimize our own. When we feel understood by another, life is meaningful and fulfilling.

Today I know I am not alone in my hardships. My own understanding of others during their difficult times helps me deal with problems of my own.

"The faults of others are like headlights on an automobile. They only seem more glaring than our own."

Anonymous

An important step in spiritual healing is when we no longer point our finger at the mistakes of others but shine the light on our own. We humbly ask our Higher Power to remove our shortcomings and are ready to work on our imperfections. As old shortcomings melt away, work associates, family and friends respond to us in new and more approving ways. We do not cling and are not attracted to clingers.

Today I am ready to have my shortcomings removed. I ask for the help I need to turn my acknowledged imperfections into better ways of thinking, feeling and being in the world.

"To a life that seizes upon content, locality seems but accident."

Elizabeth Coatsworth

Geographical escape doesn't change the way we are. We simply pack our old habits and carry them like luggage wherever we go. On the beaches of Maui, in the jungles of the Amazon or in the Grand Tetons we still have the same compulsions, feelings and mental outlooks. The surroundings are different but our responses are the same. The grass is not greener in another spot. We still have the same challenges to confront. Only by inner transformation do we make a significant change that can improve the quality of our lives.

Today I ask how I can change within to improve my life. I keep the focus on my inner development no matter where I work, reside or vacation.

"You may charge me with murder — or want of sense — (we are all of us weak at times): But the slightest approach to a false pretense was never among my crimes!"

Lewis Carroll

We fear people will not respect or accept us for who we really are, so we exaggerate our successes and hide our downfalls. False pride stands between us and our personal growth. We grow by leaps and bounds as we discard the armor of false pride and exchange hypocrisy for authenticity.

Today I let go of superiority and inferiority. I take pride in my triumphs and acknowledge my downfalls. I see myself as I truly am and let colleagues and loved ones see the true me.

"The soul of a journey is liberty, perfect liberty, to think, feel, do just as one pleases."

William Hazlitt

Independence is a gift of our spiritual search that is worth celebrating. It frees us from past beliefs and feelings that imprisoned our minds. We no longer depend on others for our worth as human beings. We are freed from people who dominated our thoughts or robbed us of our identity.

We know our minds and we follow our hearts. We take a stand on what's important to us. With this new-found independence comes freedom to make sound and responsible choices.

Today I celebrate my independence as a human being. I am free to think, feel and behave as I see fit through the divine inspiration of my inner guide.

"The merchant who for silk would sell the cotton woven in, something that is not truth will tell, and think it little sin."

George W. Bungay

There are days when we find ourselves behaving in ways that are contrary to all the spiritual progress we have made. We become discouraged. The good news is that there is encouragement in discouragement. We have learned to spot old habits as they try to sneak back into our lives, and we get better and better the longer we work at it.

Today I am encouraged by any discouraging feelings because it means I am not willing to settle for the way things used to be. I continue to follow the guide of my Higher Power and to progress in my inner search.

"For solitude sometimes is best society, and short retirement urges sweet return."

John Milton

We don't have to let our jobs rule our lives. We can take time to step out of the whirlwind of schedules and endless appointments by building time into each day for contemplation. We can meditate and let our thoughts go or stretch our emotional muscles by deep breathing, visualizing pleasant scenes, relaxing our bodies and giving ourselves positive affirmations.

Our meditations connect us to a greater source. Connection with the universal flow renews, relaxes and inspires us.

Today I keep myself connected to my Higher Power regardless of how busy or how hurried I get. Through contemplation and meditation I am ever mindful of what is truly important in my life.

"There are two days in the week about which and upon which I never worry. Two carefree days, kept sacredly free from fear and apprehension. One of the days is Yesterday. . . . And the other day I do not worry about is Tomorrow."

Robert Jones Burdette

What are the mechanics of giving up burdensome problems when they continue to haunt us? One way is to imagine ourselves putting our worries, one by one, inside a bag and setting it outside on the doorstep. As we leave for the day, we look by the doorstep and notice that the bag is gone. All of the problems were collected by our Higher Power.

Today my troubles are in the hands of my Higher Power. I put my thought and energy into things that I can control.

"Those who bring sunshine to the lives of others cannot keep it from themselves."

Sir James Matthew Barrie

Significant life changes occur through daily interactions with other people. We meet people daily in need of our compassion. Through a kind word or a helping hand, universal good flows from us to others. We can lend a caring and helping hand to someone else along the way of life's journey. Our positive thoughts and actions help others transform their lives and, in turn, improve the quality of our own.

Today I am aware that the things I say and do will affect others in my life. Inspired by my Higher Power, I lend a compassionate hand or comforting ear to someone who needs me and am blessed in return.

"Nothing on earth consumes a man more quickly than the passion of resentment."

Friedrich Wilhelm Nietzsche

Holding resentments against co-workers, friends or relatives who have harmed us is not the way to heal. We can ask ourselves what purpose hanging on to these feelings serves. Perhaps it is one way of retaliation, our way of punishing the ones who hurt us. Maybe we hold onto the old emotions because we feel sorry for ourselves.

We can set ourselves free by forgiving the wrongdoer and ourselves and releasing the resentments one by one.

Today I release all resentments that I carry. My heart refills with love and forgiveness as the burden of resentment melts away.

"*Nothing can be done at once hastily and prudently.*"

Publilius Syrus

Some of us are like pieces of popcorn on a hot plate, jumping at the heat's command. We make snap decisions and launch projects before all facts are gathered and before all options are thoroughly explored. Or we underestimate how long a job will take and then hurry to complete it. Ultimately, we spend more time cleaning up our mess because we didn't think things through.

We can make sound choices by slowing down our pace and giving them thought and reflection.

Today I think before I leap. I approach life with purpose and reflection as I make choices about the direction I go in.

" '*Twixt the optimist and pessimist the difference is droll: The optimist sees the doughnut
but the pessimist sees the hole.*"

McLandburgh Wilson

Life is like a doughnut. When we have the
entire outer ring, that's not enough for some of
us. We tell ourselves that the missing hole is the
sweetest, most delectable part.

Concentration on the hole reflects the inner
spirit. We stuff the hole with accomplishments
and achievements and continue to neglect ourselves. Optimism means looking at the whole
doughnut rather than the hole. We don't let the
missing part detract us from the ring that is
complete.

*Today I approach life optimistically. No
matter what happens I see the doughnut instead of concentrating on the hole.*

"Things are seldom what they seem, skim milk masquerades as cream."

William Schwenck Gilbert

When we live in homes where "normal" is never demonstrated, we develop fairy tale images of what they are.

In recovery we learn to distinguish the real from the unrealistic. We understand that it is okay and even healthy to disagree with another person. We begin to feel comfortable with having opposing emotions and viewpoints. We discover that living in the real world is far more satisfying than playing pretend.

Today I ask for guidance to keep my life in perspective. I do not follow the example of a fairy tale image but take a realistic view that can be just as fulfilling.

"He damned his fellows for his own unworth, and, bad himself, thought nothing good on earth."

Ambrose Bierce

We fear that if people really knew us, they'd know we were a fake. The fear of being found out drives us to work harder and harder to ensure that we are worthy of all the things we have achieved. Our feelings of unworthiness cause us to discredit ourselves and others and to view the world through negative eyes. Going within and discovering the beauty of our spiritual selves strengthens our self-worth. We can start giving ourselves and others credit where credit is due by looking on the bright side instead of harping on failure.

Today I am gratified by all the accomplishments I have made. I am learning to give myself and others the credit that is deserved.

"Much that I sought, I could not find; much that I found, I could not bind; much that I bound, I could not free; much that I freed returned to me."

Lee Wilson Dodd

Few of us are entirely free from straitjacketed lives. Our lives are like clockwork. We have a daily routine that we follow to the letter. We never divert from our schedules and never make exceptions to the rules. We call this being efficient.

Who says we cannot take a walk through the park with a friend on our lunch hour? Who says we cannot decide after work to go out to eat on the spur of the moment? We put our own limitations on our lives.

Today I look at the limits I put on myself. I loosen my life with spontaneity.

"It's not that 'today is the first day of the rest of my life,' but that now is all there is of my life."

Hugh Prather

We live in the future or we dwell in the past. We often find it difficult to pay attention to the moment. As long as we skip the present, we have no life because the past is already gone and the future never arrives. All we have is the present.

We can begin living for today and resist our mind's attempts to preoccupy us with yesterday, tomorrow or next week. From this moment we can start anew. We only have the now and we can live it to the fullest.

Today as I plan and schedule for the future, I live my life in the present. I pay attention to what happens now and discover a whole new world.

"And in his dim, uncertain sight, whatever wasn't must be right, from which it follows he had strong convictions that what was, was wrong."

Guy Wetmore Carryl

Do we silently judge others because they are not on the same path? Self-righteous attitudes of "I am always right" or "My way is the best way" have no place in recovery. We can only know what is best for ourselves, not for anyone else. Let us take our self-righteous behaviors and put them to good use on ourselves.

Today I evaluate any self-righteous attitudes. I put my energies into improving my life to the best of my ability and leave others to take care of their own.

"I have never been able to conceive how any rational being could propose happiness to himself from the exercise of power over others."

Thomas Jefferson

There is a difference in being in charge and being in control. When we're in charge, we lead through delegating, brainstorming and creative problem-solving. We allow others to have input into decisions that affect their lives. Control is a life raft that helped us survive our hectic lives up to this point. We still need this old support, but we can gradually let go of it in recovery.

Today I examine the parts of my life I compulsively control. I am learning to gradually let go of this sinking raft and to float in the direction of life my inner self takes me.

"Take your needle, my child, and work at your pattern; it will come out a rose by and by. Life is like that; one stitch at a time taken patiently, and the pattern will come out all right like embroidery."

Oliver Wendell Holmes

Because the pace is often slow and patience necessary, it helps to congratulate ourselves for the baby steps we make along the way of spiritual progress. But when we look back and see how far we have come, it's as if we have grown by leaps and bounds.

Today when I get discouraged in my spiritual journey, it is satisfying to look back and see how far I have come. I am grateful that I have reached the point of knowing and loving my inner self.

"The greatness of a man's power is the measure of his surrender."

William Booth

Our willingness to let our Higher Power guide us through our inability to control fast-paced living and excessive work habits carries over into other areas of our lives. We turn our busy habits and lives over to a greater force and watch the quality of our lives improve and our inner knowledge spiral. Worries, concerns and frustrations are resolved through self-insights and inspiration. Our willingness to change brings fulfillment and satisfaction into our lives.

Today I am willing to have changes occur in my life. I am open to the guidance of a Greater Knowing that will bring serenity and fulfillment.

". . . we are one with nature, and in harmony with the life processes. Any disharmony is a consequence of faulty perception and correctable."

Willis Harman

When we learn to dance, it is only natural that we stumble, even fall occasionally. We feel overwhelmed with the many demands made on our lives from so many outside pressures. We feel out of harmony with the world.

Spiritual progress teaches us to slow down the rhythm and pulse of our lives to a swing and style that is uniquely our own. No longer do we jump to the demands of outside pressures. We do not march to the beat of anyone's drum but our own.

Today I slow down to the rhythm and pulse of my own life. With my Higher Power as choreographer, I dance to the beat of my own drum.

"One of the most responsible things you can do as an adult is become more of a child!"

Wayne Dyer

Sometimes we get so used to moping and crying about our problems that we forget there is a flipside to life. Life is not 100 percent serious business. We can laugh at some things too. Looking at our situations in a different slant can lift the cloud of despair that hangs over our heads.

Laughter is soothing. It releases pent-up feelings. Lighthearted fun is medicine that heals an aching soul. Let's release our inner carefree child who longs to play and heal along the way.

Today I look at the lighter side of my life. I try not to take myself too seriously and I try to balance my day with humor and laughter whenever I can.

"In matters of principle, stand like a rock; in matters of taste, swim with the current."

Thomas Jefferson

How many of us muster the courage to stand up for what we believe and then back down with guilt or shame in the face of opposition? It is difficult to stand up for what we believe if we are unsure of our principles. Our inner guide helps us develop a solid platform of principles to stand on and keeps us steady and unswaying in what we believe to be right. We can ask ourselves, "What things do I believe in that I have retreated from?"

Today I will stand up for what I believe is right. I keep an open mind but am not swayed from my principles by the wants and whims of others.

"Nothing is so strong as gentleness, nothing so gentle as real strength."

St. Francis de Sales

In the work world we exhibit our strength by wielding power. We attain peak performance through aggression and competition. Our prowess reaps the rewards of fatter paychecks, prestigious positions and attractive fringe benefits. In the spiritual world our strength is recognized in more subtle ways. Spiritual enlightenment teaches us to be gentle, tender and cooperative. We reap the rewards of personal enrichment, security, serenity and fulfillment.

We achieve nothing of significance through force. A gentle approach commands more power.

Today I walk softly through my life, but my gentle spirit leaves a large footprint.

"Action may not always bring happiness; but there is no happiness without action."

Benjamin Disraeli

Some of us glide through life reacting to random events through stimulus-response like rats in a maze. We respond in predictable ways without thinking about our choices.

Spiritual enlightenment teaches us to *act* with the gift of human reasoning, not to *react* like rats in a maze. Through reacting we are controlled by people and events. When we think and then act, we make conscious choices that put us in control of our lives.

A kind word diffuses a sour attitude. Try it. It really works.

Today as I go through my routine interactions, I think about whether I am acting or reacting. I will think and then act and watch my life transform.

"And if you ever find happiness by hunting for it, you will find it, as the old woman did her lost spectacles, safe on her own nose all the time!"

Josh Billings

Are we comfortable in our own skins? Or are we always wishing we were someone else? The things that attract us to another person's lot are only what is visible to us. Hidden from us are the same emotional struggles and human frailties from which we wish to escape. Underneath the superficial trappings we are all the same. Once we accept what we have and make the best of it, we begin to feel comfortable in our own skins.

Today I appreciate being in my own skin. I accept life's challenges and feel worthy and capable of handling them.

"There are two kinds of weakness, that which breaks and that which bends."

James Russell Lowell

Sometimes our lives are so out of control, we feel like a trapeze artist flying through space. We spend enormous amounts of time and energy trying to get our feet back on the ground.

Our need for control is so important that we often over-react. But our lives are not out of control; our feelings — our reactions to the circumstances — are. The truth is that our lives are under the control of the universe. They are running as they should.

Today I am secure in my relationship with my Higher Power. My life is proceeding according to plan. My spiritual connection keeps me centered and assured when all else is flying through space.

"Blessed is he who expects nothing, for he shall never be disappointed."

Alexander Pope

When things don't go our way because of unexpected events, it naturally hurts and disappoints us. Temper tantrums express our frustration that the universe doesn't operate the way we want it to operate: We'll expect nothing, so that if nothing happens, we won't be disappointed.

We cannot eliminate disappointment from life. But we can transform how we respond to it by maturely accepting and making the best of it. In recovery we learn to accept disappointment with contentment as part of the universal condition.

Today I fully accept disappointing moments as part of the universal condition. I ask for inner guidance and maturity to make the best of what comes my way.

"To be able to find joy in another's joy, that is the secret of happiness."

George Bernanos

How often do we feel threatened when those we care about move on in their personal development? Are we so selfish and insecure that we think only of our losses and not their gains? In recovery we learn to rejoice in the good fortunes and progress of others. But our spiritual progress helps us deal with the old patterns that reside within us, so we are able to let our concern for the happiness of others over-ride our own self-centered letdowns.

Today I rejoice in the good things that happen to those I work with and love. I do not allow my own selfish feelings to interfere with my excitement and happiness for their prosperity and gain.

"He who deliberates fully before taking a step will spend his entire life on one leg."

Chinese Proverb

How content we could be if we tied up the loose ends in our personal lives. We may want to say, "I'm sorry" or "I love you" before it's too late. There may be someone we want to assure with, "It's okay. I'm here beside you." We may simply long to tenderly embrace and give emotional support to someone we love.

Today is the time to complete unfinished business. Tomorrow we or someone we care about may not be there. Tying up loose ends brings relief and serenity as the mental burden is lifted.

Today I take inventory of the overlooked details of my personal life. I right the wrongs and fill the gaps and serenity is mine.

"Good, the more communicated, more abundant grows."

John Milton

When good things start to happen to us in recovery, we often feel we do not deserve them. We have become so accustomed to struggle and heartache that we are uncomfortable with profit and happiness. We don't know how to enjoy them. We may even catch ourselves trying to sabotage our new-found good will.

In spiritual growth we learn to embrace the good that enters our lives. The more we welcome it, give thanks for it and expect it, the more will come. There is an unending supply.

Today I embrace my new way of life. I deserve all the good that comes to me and know that this is only the beginning of a never-ending supply.

"When we cannot find contentment in our-selves, it is useless to seek it elsewhere."

Francois de la Rochefoucauld

We're always telling ourselves that if certain conditions existed, that would change how we feel inside. But that's not how the universe works. No matter where we go or what happens to us, the outer conditions do not change our inner conditions. It's the other way around. Our inner thoughts and feelings change the outer conditions of our lives. We live inside ourselves. We can never escape ourselves.

Today I know I cannot escape from myself. I look within for the remedy of self-lack and discontent and find the healing I seek.

213

"It is very easy to forgive others their mistakes; it takes more grit and gumption to forgive them for having witnessed your own."

Jessamyn West

Living on the fast track leads to family neglect, insensitivity to the needs of others, suppression of love from those we really care about, rejection of anyone who cannot meet our high standards and belittlement of those who do not conduct business or bake bread as fast or in the exact way we do.

We accept our past self-righteous behaviors without guilt and commit ourselves to changing them.

Today I think about all the people I have hurt because of my fast-paced life. I will think about how I can make it up to each one of them.

"A wandering mind gathers nothing, and inattention often leads to a false move which may ruin the cause."

Richard Harris

How often are we emotionally available to those who need us? Our Higher Power speaks *to us* through other people and *through us* to other people. Every time we turn a deaf ear to a friend, we miss a chance to channel an inspirational message. We also miss an opportunity to receive spiritual nourishment. By opening our ears and hearts, we make ourselves messengers for others in need and hear all the messages that come to us through other people. We can use the messages as inspiration for our own spiritual growth.

Today I will really listen and see what others say and do. I act as a messenger for others and receive in the process.

"How rarely we weigh our neighbour in the same balance in which we weigh ourselves."

Thomas à Kempis

When we evaluate other people's character from our own slant, we get a distorted picture. We cannot feel their feelings, look through their eyes and hear the tapes playing in their brain. All of our judgments are filtered through *our* brain, *our* feelings, *our* past. We draw conclusions that are biased and usually inaccurate because they reflect *our* lives.

We can never know the thoughts and feelings of others. Our attention on them only keeps the spotlight off us.

Today I refrain from character assassination of people I know and pay attention to my own traits. I can only know my heart and head, never that of someone else.

"Those who speak most of progress measure it by quantity and not by quality."

George Santayana

Recovery is not a game where we're one up or one down. We don't compete with our colleagues and loved ones to see who can get "developed" or "fulfilled" first. True growth occurs at the rate gauged by our Higher Power, not us. We work on ourselves without comparing our progress because we cannot quantify spiritual growth. It is a process that gradually evolves at a rate unique to each of us. A measure of our true progress is a focus on our own growth, independent of anyone else's.

Today I gauge my spiritual progress by how far I have come. My progress does not compare with how much more I have to do or how much more I have done than someone else.

"Only when a man is safely ensconced under six feet of earth, with several tons of enlanding granite upon his chest, is he in a position to give advice with any certainty, and then he is silent."

Edward Newton

Trying to give the impression that we have all the answers is a type of false pride. We are so busy telling everyone how to live their lives that we don't listen to what we need to hear ourselves. When we seek humility and turn our lives over to a Higher Power, we let go of "know-it-all" attitudes. We open ourselves to spiritual enlightenment from the world around us.

Today I take inventory of my "know-it-all" attitudes. I will do more listening and less chattering, more waiting and less plowing ahead.

"*We're so engaged in doing things to achieve purposes of outer value that we forget that the inner value, the rapture that is associated with being alive, is what it's all about.*"

Joseph Campbell

How can we keep our minds on our spiritual needs when the events of the day crowd out meditation and reflection time? We have to build this time into our busy lives like everything else rather than saving it for when we have nothing better to do. As we schedule it into our day, it eventually becomes a part of our lives like mealtimes.

Today I begin building a special time in my day for contemplation, meditation and prayer. This time is as important as my other daily activities.

"He who believes himself to be far advanced in the spiritual life has not even made a good beginning."

Jean Pierre Camus

All of us are special in our own ways. Sometimes we think that we are so special that we are exempt from the laws and rules of society. Our spiritual evolvement is uplifting but it doesn't lift us above what is expected of everyone else. We are bound by the same laws and rules as everyone. True spiritual progress is when we humbly submit to these standards rather than haughtily reject them.

Today I do a humility check. I make no exceptions for myself and submit to the same set of rules and expectations by which my colleagues, friends and loved ones abide.

"The living self has one purpose only: to come into its own fullness of being, as a tree comes into full blossom, or a bird into spring beauty, or a tiger into lustre."

D. H. Lawrence

Spiritual growth is about discovering and being ourselves. It's about seeing ourselves as we really are. Once we feel comfortable with who we are without clouds of self-importance or worthlessness, we learn to be ourselves. We move through our lives without pretense and false pride and without self-neglect and self-inadequacy. It is truly an adventure and a challenge that puts meaning and purpose in our lives.

Today I am just me, no more and no less. I will be myself and let the real me shine through in all my daily interactions.

221

"A man needs self-acceptance or he can't live with himself; he needs self-criticism or others can't live with him."

James A. Pike

If someone asks us to make a list of all our character faults, we would have a long list indeed. It is so easy for us to see our shortcomings, yet so hard to see our assets. We have been shown and told of our drawbacks for so long that they stand out above all else.

Spiritual growth teaches us to see both sides of the coin — the pluses and minuses.

Today I think about my character list and strive to balance the pluses with the minuses. I think about all my strengths and give myself positive affirmations.

"No man was ever great without some portion of divine inspiration."

Marcus Tullius Cicero

We are powerless over the external world but we have inner power to make decisions and to heal ourselves. Part of spiritual growth is to admit our powerlessness and turn our will over to an inner Higher Power. But we never relinquish control of ourselves to another human being. Giving up our power to the Higher Knowing within us, paradoxically, empowers us because our lives are synchronized to the natural flow of the universe. As our lives fit into the universal scheme, and not our own, prosperity and fulfillment are ours.

Today I call upon the inspiration of my Higher Power for guidance from sunrise to nightfall. I am empowered with help to walk through life as a survivor.

"Our life is frittered away by detail . . . simplify, simplify."

Henry David Thoreau

"Keep it simple" is a term we hear a lot in recovery. Simplicity is the cornerstone of spiritual development.

Our lives become jumbled with acquiring material possessions and achieving outward success and importance. The more we try to analyze and rationalize our lives, the more complicated and crowded they become. We turn our problems over and over in our minds and worry. They grow bigger than they actually are. A simple approach to our spiritual search cuts through the complications of our everyday lives. These simple rules are: step-by-step, one day at a time and easy does it.

Today I find time for quiet contemplation. My stillness assures me of what I need to know and I enjoy the serenity that comes from it.

"Fear is never a good counselor and victory over fear is the first spiritual duty of man."

Nikolai Berdyaev

Faced with fear, how many of us turn and walk away? We are not meant to put our lives in danger but, safety precautions aside, we heal when we walk into and face our fears. When we walk the other way, fear wins the battle and continues to control us. Once we go against it, we conquer it.

Facing fear, we're trying new and challenging things that conquer old self-doubts and self-defeats. We become spiritually more fit as we see how capable we really are.

Today I do not run from my fears. As I face and walk through them, I develop greater confidence in myself and attain personal growth.

"He that commands others is not so much as free, if he doth not govern himself. The greatest performance in the life of man is the government of his spirit."

Benjamin Whichcote

Sometimes daily stresses and strains clutter our spiritual gardens and prevent us from growing. Some days the weeds of the outside world seem to grow faster than we can keep up with them and strangle our spiritual progress. Or sometimes we get so busy tending other people's gardens that weeds fill up in our own.

Our daily spiritual connections weed out life's clutter so that we grow into the beautiful people we were intended to be.

Today I am tending my own garden. I clear away weeds that have crept in while I have been busy with the outside world.

"Everything yields."

> *Ralph Waldo Emerson*

Life can be one perpetual struggle after another, one battle after another. When we feel that we are constantly battling and losing we can look at what's going on underneath. Sometimes we unconsciously draw battle lines with our combative attitudes. We try to force our will through resistance to hearing other points of view. We are argumentative, aggressive, overbearing, arrogant and self-indulgent. We create the war within ourselves without even knowing it.

Today I conduct my personal and business affairs without being combative. I take an open, positive approach to problems and reach joint decisions through cooperation rather than resistance.

"Success consists of getting up just one more time than you fall."

Oliver Goldsmith

Life is full of ups and downs. Understanding and dealing with this fundamental truth is part of recovery.

There are good times and bad times, highs and lows, joys and sadness. We get hired and fired. We get recognized and overlooked, we get loved and rejected and we get credit and blame. Sometimes we feel great and other times small.

Knowing we cannot change the ups and downs of life but that we can only adjust our inner selves to them brings healing.

Today I am strapped in for the ups and downs in my life. I know they will come and faith in my Higher Power keeps me prepared.

"Mere silence is not wisdom, for wisdom consists in knowing when and how to speak and when and where to keep silent."

                                    Albert Camus

We are often compelled to give our opinions and comments, even when unsolicited. There are times when saying nothing is the best solution. We neither condemn nor condone, approve nor disapprove. The condition may not even need our commentary or may not be worth our agony and energy. The predicament may resolve itself with greater ease without our input. Sometimes silence speaks louder than words. Knowing when to speak and when to hold our tongues is a leap in growth.

Today I consciously choose when to use silence and when to use words. I will be aware of what happens when I silently listen rather than talk.

"Man must cease attributing his problems to his environment, and learn again to exercise . . . his personal responsibility in the realm of faith and morals."

Albert Schweitzer

How often do we solve problems by forcing solutions that don't fit? Nobody *makes* us sick, angry or nervous. This is another way of making ourselves victims of life rather than survivors. Our emotions are our own making. Facing problems and owning them when they are truly ours help us become responsible for our feelings and actions. Being responsible for our feelings rather than blaming others puts us further down the road of healing.

Today, however I feel, it's because I choose it. Nobody made me think, feel or do anything.

"*At bottom every man knows well enough that he is a unique being, only once on this earth; and by no extraordinary chance will such a marvelously picturesque piece of diversity in unity as he is, ever be put together a second time.*"

Friedrich Wilhelm Nietzsche

Each of us is unique. No one will ever experience life in exactly the same way. No one else will have the same chance to help another person who needs help at that instant and to teach the people who need to learn something at that second. How lucky we are to have this once in a lifetime chance to live our lives in our own unique way! How exciting to be alive!

Today I am grateful for who I am. I do not take my uniqueness for granted, but am awed by the wonder of it all.

"To get nearer to God, you have to get further and further away from 'I', 'my', 'me', and 'mine'."

Meher Baba

Overuse of the "I" or its derivatives such as "my," "me" or "mine" is a reflection of how self-centered we can become. As long as our minds are stuck on ourselves, we are stuck in the healing process. Sometimes to grow we need to let others have the spotlight. Showing an interest in the problems and needs of others is the hallmark of spiritual awareness. Life is about sharing and giving everyone equal opportunity for growth.

Today I think about how I occupy center stage. Is my life one giant monologue or is there dialogue in the script?

"If you constantly think of illness, you eventually become ill; if you believe yourself to be beautiful, you become so."

Shakti Gawain

Everything that happens is a thought before it is an action. Artists create their masterpieces in their minds before putting them on canvas. The writer and musician have the thoughts of their compositions before they write them.

When we think negative things about a situation, we're already creating the tone the action will take. When we visualize positive things, we create positive outcomes of situations.

Today I use my thoughts to create positive outcomes in my life. I will think constructive thoughts and radiate positive energy to my associates.

"Perfection does not consist in lacerating or killing the body, but in killing our perverse self-will."

St. Catherine of Siena

Admitting our powerlessness and letting go of self-will brings many of the emotions we experience in bereavement. Denial is the first. Our resistance makes us try to bargain our way out of letting go. But our Higher Power doesn't bargain. We may become depressed when none of the tactics work. Finally we understand that acceptance is the way to grow spiritually.

When we grieve over self-will, we essentially mourn the death of the "old me." Mourning the old and celebrating the new helps us heal ourselves.

Today I say goodbye to self-will and hello to surrender. I am reborn into a new life of spiritual recovery.

"We are not our own, any more than what we possess is our own. We did not make ourselves; we cannot be supreme over ourselves. We cannot be our own masters. We are God's property by creation, by redemption, by regeneration."

John Henry Newman

As we grow with each new day, we are like potter's clay, taking more form as we are pounded and molded. The form we take is not our own and we often don't understand the form things are taking. There are times when we want to be our own pot, so we try to mold ourselves in our own image. Our interference makes a complete mess. Only through faith that we are turning out to be a beautiful piece of work can we remain the clay and not try to become our own pot.

Today I surrender to the potter's wheel of my Higher Power. I feel myself taking perfect form with each new day.

"The world is wide; with God for guide I need not hide nor flee. My destined course shall be the source of immortality."

                                        Robert Lee Straus

When we're going somewhere, we need proper guidance to get there. We need to know where we're going and we need instruments to keep us on track. Many of us launch out in life without direction. We think we know where we are going, that we don't need help getting there. We end up lost and confused. With inner guidance, when we take a wrong turn or get lost, our Higher Power puts us back on track.

Today I consult my inner guide to keep me on my path. I feel confident and serene that I am headed where I need to go.

"He is never less at leisure than when at leisure."

Marcus Tullius Cicero

By overplanning and overorganizing our lives for 24 hours a day, we make them predictable and eliminate the unknown and uncertainty. Or so we think.

Packing our daily lives full of busy tasks and commitments is an escape, pure and simple. We do it out of fear. During idle hours, we feel out of control. But no matter how hard we try, we can never control our lives. With our Higher Power in control, we are free to enjoy the moment and live more flexibly.

Today I refrain from packing my life too full of activities and projects. I save plenty of time for enjoying the now and for quiet meditation.

"The problem of distinguishing what we are and what we are not responsible for in this life is one of the greatest problems of human existence. It is never completely solved; for the entirety of our lives we must continually assess and reassess where our responsibilities lie in the ever-changing course of events."

M. Scott Peck

By taking continual stock of where we went wrong from day to day and admitting it, we grow stronger and stronger. Fulfillment and serenity are ours as we constantly evaluate our daily lives.

Today I take quiet stock of my mistakes. I am learning to admit my wrongs and feel the peace and serenity that come from this action.

"Consider how hard it is to change yourself and you'll understand what little chance you have of trying to change others."

Jacob M. Braude

Resistance to what comes our way only keeps us agitated and upset. Acceptance gives us peace of mind. We don't have to accept others' insults. But we can accept the fact that we cannot change their behavior. Accepting our feelings for what they are keeps us from denying the truth in our lives. We created these feelings anyway and we can uncreate them. Accepting things as they are is the first step to serenity and the courage to change those parts of our lives that are changeable.

Today I accept the things I cannot change. I ask for courage to change the things I can and the wisdom to know the difference between the two.

"Since modern man experiences himself both as the seller and the commodity to be sold on the market, his self-esteem depends on conditions beyond his control. If he is 'successful,' he is valuable; if he is not, he is worthless."

Erich Fromm

People cannot fill our inner void. Neither can material possessions, nor any of our addictions. Inner emptiness stems from spiritual hunger. Going within and connecting with our inner guide through prayer and meditation fills up the empty hole.

Today when I feel empty inside, I know it is time for a spiritual refill. Through prayer and meditation, I am able to fill this inner hole.

"People who fly into a rage always make a bad landing."

Will Rogers

Anger is a natural emotion. It's how we deal with our anger that makes a difference in our lives.

When we're angry, we can yell and scream, rant and rave or maturely express our views. Sometimes we use our anger like a steamroller to run people down who get in our way. We've learned that when we do this, others retreat and we get our way.

There is a strength in gentleness. Resolving our anger in a mature way is a sign of spiritual growth.

Today I ask myself why I am angry and how I express my anger. I will find mature ways of dealing with my feelings.

"Shame is one of the major destructive forces in all human life. In naming shame, I began to have power over it."

John Bradshaw

We learn shame through words, stares or scowls. Shame is the scab on our inner wounds that never heals. Superachieving, overeating, co-dependent relationships and other addictions drive us to heal the shame. But it continues to fester despite compulsive and addictive behaviors. As we learn to accept and love ourselves exactly as we are, the scab of shame begins to heal.

Today I name shame for the destructive force it is. As I release it from my mind and heart, I gain power over it and over my ability to live more fully.

"It is tragic how few people ever 'possess their souls' before they die. . . . Most people are other people. Their thoughts are someone else's opinions, their lives a mimicry, their passions a quotation."

Oscar Wilde

When we live our lives afraid of what others will think, we never really live them as we see fit. We live out of fear rather than out of self-satisfaction. The only way to achieve true happiness is to live our lives according to our own inner values and beliefs. It means we develop our own standards of acceptance.

Today I live my life by my own internal standards. I am not bent and swayed by what other people think but feel comfortable with my inner sense of who I am.

"Guilt is the prosecutor who knows how to make every victim feel like the criminal."

Ruth Gendler

Guilty is a verdict that we often render on ourselves for the smallest offense. No matter what we do, there's always something for which we must punish ourselves.

Guilt is self-defeating and self-destructive. It has no place in spiritual recovery, for we use guilt to condemn ourselves and others. As we release these unhealthy feelings, we learn the power of self-love. Acquitting ourselves by rendering a verdict of not guilty frees us to live our lives fully.

Today I release myself from the prison of guilt. I pardon myself for past mistakes, accept and love myself fully and let guilty feelings go.

*"Made direct amends to such people wher-
ever possible, except when to do so would injure
them or others."*

Step 9, Alcoholics Anonymous

Now is the time to ask forgiveness of all the
people we have hurt through our hurry and
neglect. Making amends is done out of desire
and commitment, not out of guilt or obligation.
One of the best ways is to change old behaviors. During the amendment process, we suddenly realize that the little child inside of us
has grown up and that we are more mature and
responsible adults. We have restored our self-
respect and the respect of others.

*Today I make amends by changing old
behaviors into new, more considerate and
caring ones. As I participate in the amendment process, I grow up and mature.*

"It is better to know nothing than to know what ain't so."

Henry Wheeler Shaw

Each day of inner reflection brings greater clarity. We begin to see ourselves as we truly are. We see our strong points and areas for improvement. We set goals based on our capabilities. We acknowledge our setbacks. We live by our inner standards of right and wrong and attempt to please no one but ourselves. False pride no longer serves us, neither does self-condemnation.

Clarity comes from hard spiritual toil. No addiction or possession can match the joy and serenity that comes from clarity.

Today I ask for clarity, without self-deception, in all my affairs. I am ready for the peace and serenity it brings.

"As we grow into higher consciousness, we discover that it is more important to be the right person than to find the right person."

Ken Keyes

Everybody needs boundaries to grow. Boundaries tell us how far we can go. They keep us from overstepping our bounds. Boundaries keep us mentally safe and healthy in our growth and development.

They allow us to keep our individuality and uniqueness. Boundaries help us to own our feelings and thoughts, to accept responsibility for our mistakes. Boundaries don't keep people out; they let them know how far in they can come.

Today I define my boundaries by exercising my individuality and independence. I will use my boundaries to be the genuine person I am.

"It is with narrow-minded people as with narrow-necked bottles; the less they have in them, the more noise they make in pouring it out."

Alexander Pope

A narrow mind doesn't have room to grow. It keeps us self-centered. No ideas or customs or ways are entertained if they are not already familiar to us. We are closed.

When we close out new ways of thinking and doing, we shut ourselves down. Only through an open mind do we receive the gift of recovery.

Today I don't let narrow-mindedness keep me from growing. I keep myself open to new experiences with each new day.

"To escape criticism — do nothing, say nothing, be nothing."

Elbert Hubbard

Taking a chance is a pre-condition for spiritual growth. We have to cross the bridge to get to the other side of the valley. We have to go through the dark tunnel to get through the mountain. We have to cross the busy intersection to get to the other side of the street.

Spiritual progress comes from effort — from going over, through and across the avenues that are provided to us. On the other side, we gain rewards unmatched by human complacency.

Today I don't let vulnerability block my personal growth. I take a chance on life as I take action in healing myself.

"Nothing great was ever achieved without enthusiasm."

Ralph Waldo Emerson

We owe it to ourselves to approach life with enthusiasm. It puts us in forward gear and gives us a spark to move.

We can approach our work with enthusiasm just as easily as we can with dread. We can enthusiastically keep a dreaded commitment just as well as showing reluctance. We can drive to work in a thunderstorm with the same enthusiasm that we drive with on a sunny day.

The fire of enthusiasm can be rekindled by sheer willingness on our part. The quality of life takes on a glow we've never before seen.

Today I get in touch with the enthusiastic part of myself. I approach my day with enthusiasm and a zest for living.

"God helps them that help themselves."

Benjamin Franklin

We cannot buy inner healing, no matter how much money or power we have. Like all things of value, healing is priceless and hard to get. It is attainable only through hard work, persistence and effort. The only person who can get it for us is ourselves. We have the tools and our inner guides to help us but we must do the work. No one can do that for us.

We earn the benefits of personal healing by living a program and the payoff is invaluable. A little effort on our part goes a long way.

Today I will put effort into my spiritual growth. I will put into practice all the things I learn as I live my life fully.

"One of the weaknesses of our age is our apparent inability to distinguish our needs from our greeds."

Don Robinson

We want to make our mark in life before we die. In the material world, we gauge our mark by how much money we make and how many possessions we can buy. Marks are made by landing a high-paying, high-powered job, trendy clothes, fashionable homes and expensive cars.

These marks, however, are fleeting. Material gain has no lasting value. We can truly make a mark by putting our attention and energy into our inner human value.

Today I make my mark through human virtue. I share my inner worth through my deeds and spread the wealth for a lifetime.

> *"Loneliness is such an omnipotent and painful threat to many persons that they have little conception of the positive values of solitude, and even at times are frightened at the prospect of being alone."*

> *Rollo May*

We can be surrounded by people and feel a deep yearning that stems from an inner emptiness. We try to resolve it by staying busy and filling our lives with things to do.

We're empty inside because of self-isolation. We can fill that lonely spot by getting acquainted with ourselves. When we have ourselves, we don't yearn for anyone else.

Today I embrace loneliness. I discover that I can never truly be lonely in the company of myself and my Higher Power.

"There lives more faith in honest doubt, believe me, than in half the creeds."

Alfred Lord Tennyson

We want to know that a car is dependable before we invest our money. When we launch our spiritual search, we want proof that we'll get a payoff from our investment of time and energy. We listen to and read about what others say of their own spiritual healing to decide if it is worthwhile. We want a dependable path before we sink our teeth into it. We want a written guarantee.

When we spend our time looking for evidence, we miss the experience along the way. Faith comes before recovery. It is a wonderful gift that develops slowly.

Today I have faith in the healing process. Even when things don't go my way, I hold strong convictions that my life is working according to plan.

"Nature is always kind enough to give even her clouds a humorous lining."

James Russell Lowell

Living life truthfully requires us to be as open to humor and amusement as we are to pain and sorrow. But some of us take life's challenges so seriously that we think our spiritual growth has to be all work and no play. Too few of us laugh or smile on the job and we feel guilty having fun at work. We believe that laughter and fun are exceptions to the rule of getting the job done. Often we forget to laugh at ourselves and see the humorous side of life. The potential for fun and happiness is all around us. A dash of humor adds spice to humdrum everyday life.

Today I look for the amusing side of life. I let humor do its work in my life to brighten my path.

"To have a thing is nothing, if you've not the chance to show it, and to know a thing is nothing, unless others know you know it."

Lord Nancy

Compliments are sometimes hard to accept, especially when we cannot acknowledge the good in ourselves. We often find it easier to accept negative comments and put-downs because they more closely match our self-images. Many of us, because we are so used to criticism, feel more comfort with it than with praise.

Seeing ourselves truthfully includes acknowledging and affirming all the good things about ourselves. Accepting compliments is a way of accepting the truth about ourselves.

Today I am learning to see myself more truthfully. That includes accepting the positive views others have of me.

"Nothing is at last sacred but the integrity of your mind."

Ralph Waldo Emerson

We pretend that we are powerful decision makers, that we have all the answers, that we are unruffled by hurtful things people say, that we are calm in the face of turmoil and that we don't need anyone else in our lives.

Deep inside, we know that this is not true at all. It's only an act we perform to get through the business of the day. Admitting to ourselves how we really feel, we receive the gift of integrity. We are fulfilled when we embrace our true selves.

Today I don't have to hide from myself or pretend to be someone I'm not. I experience this day as I truly am, with honor and integrity.

"Don't make yourself so big. You are not so small."

Jewish Proverb

Humility is the light we use for inner exploration. It is an honest evaluation of who we are in our relationship to others. Without humility we do not have the vision essential for spiritual growth.

There are steps to humility that can be taken one by one. First comes acknowledging our powerlessness and then turning our will over to a Higher Power. Next we acknowledge our faults and are prepared to have them removed. Then we humbly ask our Higher Power to remove our shortcomings. Our old hurts and habits are healed.

Today humility lights up my life. I am not afraid to look at myself as I truly am and to let it shine on myself and others.

"Emergencies have always been necessary to progress. It was darkness which produced the lamp. It was fog that produced the compass. It was hunger that drove us to exploration. And it took a depression to teach us the real value of a job."

Victor Hugo

We never truly reach a dead end in our search. Snags are only temporary delays put there to help us grow spiritually. When we face occasional barricades, we discover that there is always a new path to take. When we hit snags on our journey, we don't throw in the towel. When life sets up roadblocks, we grow enormously by taking detours.

Today I remember that occasional snags are part of the trip. I look for new ways when I am delayed in my journey.

"The nurse of full-grown souls is solitude."

James Russell Lowell

As the pounding surf erodes the seashore, the wear and tear of daily living can erode our spirits. Daily commitments keep us awash in a sea of errands, appointments and job commitments.

We can always find time for ourselves. There's always a place for us once we stop denying our worth. Time for ourselves replenishes the soil that we felt slipping away from underneath our feet. We become a sea wall of strength against the push and pull of daily tides.

Today I think about the spiritual erosion in my life. I will put back the parts of me that have slowly drifted away with the hustle and bustle of the outside world.

"Now is all we have. Everything that has ever happened to you and anything that is ever going to happen to you, is just a thought."

Wayne Dyer

Many of us cart around hurtful childhood experiences that keep our adult lives from working. When we allow unresolved hurts to interfere with our lives, we repel others.

We can heal these hurts by touching our inner child. We see that the pain is in the past, not the present, and we need not use the same dysfunctional ways of responding as children. We are adults now. Once we abdicate old feelings and hurts, we begin to attract people into our lives, rather than push them away.

Today I do not let the past contaminate my present. I live with a fresh, clean slate and open myself to healthier and happier change.

"Worry does not empty tomorrow of its sorrow; it empties today of its strength."

Corrie Ten Boom

Spiritual growth is not about staying put. It's about change and moving forward. We want to heal ourselves but we keep ourselves anchored in one spot with worry. The bonds of worry weigh us down and bring us to our knees, preventing us from moving forward on our spiritual path.

In recovery we learn that worry is self-defeating. Our burdens are lifted and we learn to put our thoughts and energies to better use on our spiritual healing.

Today I accept the things over which I have no control. I anchor myself with worry less and sail with serenity more.

"An intelligent plan is the first step to success. Planning is the open road to one's destination. If one doesn't know where he is going, how can he expect to get there?"

Charles Moore

A little forethought saves all of us trouble down the road. Those of us on the fast track find ourselves taking the quick fix to problems. The results can be disastrous. Forethought helps us set goals and figure out how we can arrive at them. Thoughtful preparation gives us a more direct path than mindless floundering and saves us from going back and cleaning up a mess.

Part of living in the present includes preparation for the future. Setting goals and planning ahead help make our journey smooth and direct.

Today I use forethought in planning my future affairs. I live only for today but plan for tomorrow.

"It is better to be alone than in bad company."

George Washington

As we make significant changes in our personal growth, some long-time friendships fall by the wayside along with many of our old habits. But we find new, perhaps healthier friendships to replace the old ones. Sometimes it's sad to let go of old friends but it may be necessary. Our friendships are a reflection of who we are inside. When we make a spiritual transformation, we are different from the old self. Healthier relationships are part of a trade for a healthier way of being.

Today I do not let old relationships hold me back from personal growth. I value friendships — either new or old — that reflect the new me.

"People seldom want to walk over you until you lie down."

Elmer Wheeler

Expressing intimacy teaches us the difference between establishing boundaries and erecting barricades. Sometimes as we drop our barricades, we drop our boundaries too and get involved in co-dependent relationships. Without our boundaries, we are just as isolated as we were with our barricades.

Spiritual progress teaches us to gradually remove the barricades while keeping the boundaries. We share ourselves with other people but we keep our self-respect and individuality.

Today I learn the difference between opening myself up and making myself a doormat. As I practice intimacy, I maintain my own person while sharing myself with others.

"It is vain to hope to please all alike. Let a man stand with his face in what direction he will, he must necessarily turn his back on one-half of the world."

William Feather

No matter how hard we try, there will always be someone who doesn't like or approve of something we do. But that doesn't mean we are wrong and they are right or that we are right and they are wrong. Their feedback may give us a chance to rethink our point of view or to reaffirm our own stance. In either case we remain our own person with integrity and convictions.

Today I do not seek approval; I seek friendships. I am open to disapproval for re-evaluating my actions but I do not allow it to shape my character.

"Let every tub stand on its own bottom."

John Bunyan

We have lived in chaos and conflict for so long that we often feel more comfortable with it than with tranquility. Even today we may find it difficult to evade conflict. As long as we allow others' dysfunction to entrap us, we stay sick. Spiritual progress teaches us to continue our healing process at all costs, for if we are not mentally healthy, we can do no good for others. Through detachment we keep an emotional distance from the dysfunction that surrounds us and threatens to engulf us.

Today I offer my help to others but do not participate in their dysfunction. My search for tranquility gets priority over controversy and dissension.

"Anger is often more hurtful than the injury that caused it."

American Proverb

Anger is like an insidious cancer that slowly eats away at our insides. It blurs our judgment and clouds our emotions. As we backpack its weight around with us, anger gives us an excuse to unleash it when things don't go our way.

Perhaps we have a lot to be angry about; but acknowledging our anger does not condone angry outbursts. It merely recognizes the truth of what's there. Once acknowledged and re-solved, the seething stops.

Today I acknowledge the unresolved anger I've backpacked. I release the anger and feel the healing process begin to work.

"I never found the companion that was so companionable as solitude."

Henry David Thoreau

Being alone is something we avoid at all costs. We run from solitude and fill our lives with doing and possessing to keep lonely feelings at bay.

Solitude is to be avoided only when we are afraid of what we will find lurking inside ourselves. We can change our outlook of solitude from one of loneliness to one of connecting with our spiritual selves. Solitude bridges the gap between the physical and spiritual worlds and is one of the greatest joys of recovery.

Today I welcome solitude and being alone for meditation and reflection. I value aloneness and welcome it for my spiritual growth.

"On every level of life from housework to heights of prayer, in all judgment and all efforts to get things done, hurry and impatience are sure marks of the amateur."

Evelyn Underhill

We're so accustomed to speeding from task to task that lulls or waiting conflicts with our engine speed. We expect the people and situations we come into contact with to adapt to our hurried pace.

Fast-track living keeps us speeding through our lives until we eventually fizzle out. Slowing down and seeking quiet contemplation and connections with our spiritual guide overhauls our engines.

Today I overhaul my engine by slowing down my pace. I do not expect the universe to accelerate to match my engine speed but I slow mine down to fit it.

"An optimist goes to the window every morning and says, 'Good morning, God.' The pessimist goes to the window and says, 'Good God, morning!' "

Anonymous

At first the tourist was smitten by the beauty of the country. But after a week the beauty of the towns was marred by his attention to garbage in the river and cracks in the pavement. When we relive one day as if it's our first, our lives are transformed. We have a deeper appreciation for who we are and for what we have. We gain a stronger bond with co-workers and loved ones that perhaps we took for granted. Let's ask ourselves, "Do we look for cracks in the pavement or pay attention to where the street takes us?"

Today I expect to be awestruck as I experience my life through fresh eyes. I am deeply appreciative of my life and the people in it.

"If you wish to travel far and fast, travel light. Take off all your envies, jealousies, unforgiveness, selfishness and fears."

Glenn Clark

Wallowing in self-pity is just another way of placing ourselves as victims of life. It allows us to blame others for our plight and lets us off the responsibility hook but gives our power away to other people and situations. We create outcomes that make us victims rather than survivors.

Our spiritual path teaches us that we can overcome any situation by taking action and by giving up self-defeating thoughts.

Today I do not indulge in self-pity when things don't work out. I accept responsibility for situations as a survivor, not as a victim of life.

"A prejudice is a vagrant opinion without visible means of support."

Ambrose Bierce

When we believe we are inferior or inadequate, we imprison ourselves. Constantly proving ourselves, putting ourselves last or doing what others want are additional bars on the prison cell we build around us. We imprison others in the same way when we hold prejudices that limit them by sex, religion, race or social status. How tragic to live our lives without seeing the truth about ourselves and others! How exhilarating to free ourselves of destructive, mental restrictions!

Today I look at any restrictions I have placed on myself or others because of my own prejudices. I try to keep myself open to the human potential of everyone in my life, myself included.

"To pretend to satisfy one's desires by possession is like using straw to put out a fire."

Chinese Proverb

We possess things; we love people. Too few of us follow this advice. How many of us, in fact, follow the reverse? We possess people; we love things. The healing process teaches us that we don't own people and we can never possess them. Ownership gives us a feeling of power and control, the need for which comes from our own deep insecurities. Attaining inner harmony extinguishes the need to possess things or people. Serenity from knowing that we are complete reduces our need to own anyone or anything.

Today I do not need possessions to make me secure in my life. I am already complete and the possession of another person or thing does not satisfy an inner need.

"Continued to take personal inventory and, when we were wrong, promptly admitted it."

Step 10, Alcoholics Anonymous

Once we have made amends to people we have harmed, we don't sit back on our laurels because spiritual transformation is a lifetime commitment. We are involved in an ongoing process of self-discovery as we continue to take personal inventory. Self-examination, admitting mistakes and imperfections, and allowing others to make mistakes become daily habits. We forgive and are kinder to ourselves and others. We understand that no one ever arrives at perfection and that life is a series of lessons and mistakes from which to learn.

Today I continue to take personal inventory and, when wrong, promptly admit it. Although I know I'll never be perfect, I learn from my mistakes and become the best person I can.

"We must be anchored in self-discipline if we are to venture successfully in freedom."

Harold E. Kohn

If we think of our lives as a jigsaw puzzle, we may have everybody else's pieces squarely in place. Going into the office early, staying late, working weekends may be the first pieces we fit into life's puzzle.

But what about the missing pieces of our lives that complete our puzzle? What about time for ourselves, for play and for our families? It takes self-discipline to complete our jigsaw puzzle. It helps us pick up the pieces of our lives.

Discipline keeps us consistent and focused in our personal development.

Today I work on completing my jigsaw puzzle. I look for the missing parts and discipline myself to include them on a daily basis.

"A truth that's told with bad intent beats all the lies you can invent."

William Blake

Denial prevents us from seeing our lives as they truly are because we cannot let go of old dysfunctional thoughts. We have our pet refrains such as, "I don't mind" and "Things are not that bad" that protect us from the truth.

Denial of our needs, compulsions and problems does not make the truth go away. Wiping out denial in our lives is the first step to breaking the barriers that prevent personal growth. We can take an honest look at our addiction to fast-track living, compulsive overachieving, co-dependent relationships or drug abuse.

Today I think about my refusal to see my life as it truly is. I take a more honest look each time I question my denial of the truth.

"You know I say just what I think, and nothing more nor less; I cannot say one thing and mean another."

Henry Wadsworth Longfellow

Many of us say yes when we'd like to say no. Fear of saying no comes from fear of rejection by others. We put our likes and desires behind those of others and, as a result, our needs never get met.

Saying no means we're taking care of ourselves by honestly asserting our opinions and choices. When we are honest with ourselves and others, we feel better about ourselves, our needs get met and the self-contempt vanishes.

Today I am learning to say no when I mean no. I find that I like myself much better and others do too, when I assert my honest views.

"It is one of the most beautiful compensations of this life that no man can sincerely try to help another without helping himself."

Ralph Waldo Emerson

As we let go of old habits, thoughts and feelings, we make ourselves receptive to life's spiritual riches. As good comes to us, we must let go of it in order to keep it. The negative traits of hoarding, possessing and gluttony block the channels of receptivity. Only by letting go of greedy and selfish ways can our spiritual progress continue. As we give, we receive. Sharing our thoughts and feelings with those who are downtrodden helps them and us grow by leaps and bounds.

Today I share both my spiritual and material good with others. As I reveal myself to others and let go of my abundance, I continue to prosper from life's blessings.

"Little things affect little minds."

Benjamin Disraeli

The light bulb burns out in the bathroom while we get ready for work. The car has a flat tire on the way to the market. The television is on the blink. "The house is falling apart!" we scream. Little things. When we find ourselves overreacting to life's small events, it reflects our inability to accept the way the world operates. Once we see how trivial little things are in the grand scheme of things, we act rather than react. We accept them as a small part of life, they fail to dominate our emotions and we go about our day.

Today when little things go wrong, I don't make more of them than they are. I know this will happen from time to time and learn to roll with the punches.

"The rung of a ladder was never meant to rest upon, but only to hold a man's foot long enough to enable him to put the other somewhat higher."

Thomas Huxley

Climbing the corporate ladder is successful when we take our spiritual selves along for the ascent. Otherwise, we get to the top and there's nothing there but loneliness and emptiness. Climbing together keeps us connected to the true essence of success: self-knowledge and spiritual awareness. Daily spiritual contact lets us keep our sights on the heavens and our feet firmly on the ground.

Today as I compete in the business world, I stay grounded by constant spiritual contact. I take precious time each day to connect with my inner guide so I have plenty of company on my way up.

"Only love can bring individual beings to their perfect completion as individuals because only love takes possession of them and unites them by what lies deepest within them."

Pierre Teilhard de Chardin

Closeness is difficult when we've been betrayed or we feel inadequate or shameful. It becomes very difficult for us to share ourselves because of past hurts. But we can heal our intimate selves. Self-love is the beginning of intimacy. When we heap love and caring on ourselves, we begin to heal our inner hurts. Self-love opens us up to the love of others. We no longer fear revealing the genuine self that has received tender, loving care.

Today I heal my intimate self by loving myself fully. I open myself up to giving and receiving love without fear or shame.

"All the beautiful sentiments in the world weigh less than a single lovely action."

James Russell Lowell

Sharing our feelings with others has a ripple healing effect. We are healed and those with whom we share our feelings benefit from our shared experience.

A kind deed, a caring telephone call, a card to someone convalescing, a hug and a kiss are ways of passing our love around. Taking time out of our busy day to love ourselves and someone else keeps the feeling reverberating like ripples on a pond. The circle widens and our sharing spreads, enriching our lives.

Today I share my feelings with someone else who will benefit by them. As I send out my caring, I heal myself and help others in their own healing process.

"Necessary, forever necessary, to burn out false shames and smelt the heaviest ore of the body into purity."

D. H. Lawrence

We feel disgraced by the actions of others and riddle ourselves with shame. But we cannot take responsibility for the actions of others no matter how close we are to them. Once we give up our need to be responsible for what other people do, we give up shame we voluntarily wore. Relinquishing shame purges us of needless self-hate and contributes to our spiritual recovery.

Today I take responsibility for my behavior and mine alone. I do not wear the mantle of shame for others because I did not cause, cannot cure and cannot change their actions.

"Ne'er look for birds of this year in the nests of the last."

Miguel de Cervantes

Many of us have insulated our feelings, sealed them away into a time capsule. Tragically, some of us never break the seal but spiritual healing requires us to open the capsule and examine its contents. Once we do, we discover feelings of yesteryear still influencing us today.

Do we see pity or shame? Is there self-hate or false pride? These old feelings are interesting artifacts to examine and to discover how far we have come in our new lives.

Today I study the thoughts and feelings that I sealed away in the darker corners of my mind. I keep what still serves me and put the others back.

"When you shake your fist at someone, remember that all your fingers are pointing at yourself."

Jacob Braude

Sometimes it's the people who love us the most on whom we dump our hostility when it is actually intended for a co-worker, client or the boss. We find it more comfortable to punish the ones we love because they are more likely to tolerate our anger.

In recovery we don't need targets on which to direct our anger. We can now go within and solve our feelings without drawing innocent people into our guerilla warfare.

Today I put away my weapons and realize there's nothing to defend when I'm honest with myself. I express my feelings to the real targets and not to innocent bystanders.

"Keep your hands open, and all the sands of the desert can pass through them. Close them, and all you can feel is a bit of grit."

                                        Taisen Deshimaru

There is a difference between stubbornness and persistence. Stubbornness is another expression of self-will to have things as we want them to be, not as they are. When we stubbornly refuse to give in, we resist the truth. We are persistent when we are right and we look for new ways to achieve our purpose. As we let go and let God, our spiritual channels are cleared of stubborn resistance and opened with dogged persistence.

Today I do not let stubborn resistance clutter my path. I am persistent in my spiritual journey and open to the truth.

"Time is but the stream I go a-fishing in."

Henry David Thoreau

"There are just not enough hours in a day" is our constant refrain. Our need to put more hours in a day is a reflection of our need to overdo, our inability to accept what *is* and to live our lives within the universal framework. Our lives start working as we structure our days for only 24 hours. We are less stressed, just as productive and have time for spiritual reflection each day. We deflate our days with less doing and lighten them with more being.

Today I work on deflating my day from 30 hours of doing to 24 hours of doing and being. As I accept only 24 hours in a day, I am less frustrated and more fulfilled.

"A child's world is fresh and new and beautiful, full of wonder and excitement. It is our misfortune that for most of us that clear-eyed vision, that true instinct for what is beautiful and awe-inspiring, is dimmed and even lost before we reach adulthood."

Rachel Carson

Many times as an experience becomes familiar to us, we lose the fresh outlook we once had. Turning dislikes into preferences and negativity into positiveness can literally transform our mental outlook. This practice keeps life fresh and keeps us from being bored with it. It develops within us a deeper appreciation for the blessings we have.

Today I experience my life through fresh eyes. I find that as I do this my days are richer and fuller and I am more content with my world.

"Gather ye rosebuds while ye may, Old Time is still a-flying, and this same flower that smiles today, tomorrow will be dying."

Robert Herrick

Carpe diem is Latin for "seize the day." In our spiritual search this expression reminds us to live in the now because the present is the most valuable time we can ever have. It advises us to live our lives fully, not fretting about what went wrong or worrying about what will happen.

As we think of our own mortality and how fleeting life is, many things come to mind that need doing. Today is the day to tell someone we love them, make a confession or mend a relationship. We seize the day to do the undone.

Today I appreciate my life and how elusive it is. I think of many undone things that need doing and seize the day to live it fully.

"Flow with whatever may happen and let your mind be free: Stay centered by accepting whatever you are doing. This is the ultimate."

Chuang Tzu

Life is not tailored to human specifications and it does not bend to fit each lifestyle. The universe has operated by its own laws since the beginning of time and doesn't change for any of us. Still, we try to make our lives work as we want them to by our rules. The key to personal fulfillment is accepting life exactly as it is and living our lives within these boundaries.

Today I ride in the direction the universe is going. As I give up trying to have things my way, my life runs smoother than ever before and happiness and serenity are mine.

"Americans generally spend so much time on things that are urgent *that we have none left to spend on those that are* important."

Henry Ward Beecher

Spiritual growth is not about bare existence; it's about living fully. Some of us live shipwrecked lives in our world of plenty. We spend our waking hours surviving rather than living. Our inner guide is like a hidden tutor. We are still learning the rules of life and are being constantly tutored by a Higher Knowing that sustains us through daily challenges. Without our inner guide we can survive life but we cannot live it fully.

Today I make sure that I have the bare essentials to live my life fully, not just to exist in it. My inner guide sustains me through every trial and tribulation.

"The urge to transcend self-conscious self-hood is a principal appetite of the soul."

Aldous Huxley

Self-centeredness makes us self-seeking. Everything revolves around us and our needs and we have little empathy for others. We do things for others only in exchange for what it will bring us. Self-centeredness keeps us stuck; self-love propels us forward. Once we love ourselves, we move beyond it to sharing ourselves with others. Self-love allows us to care for others and do kind deeds without the need for payoff or recognition. We give for the sheer joy of giving. Human compassion and kindness come naturally with self-love.

Today I distinguish between self-love and self-centeredness. I work on loving myself and extending that love through thoughtfulness and caring for others.

"Though you may get lost for a time, eventually your inner heart will hear what to do and all the impurities in your world will just become grist for the mill."

Ram Dass

It is a challenge to transform daily experiences into useful rather than damaging consequences. Making something out of nothing doesn't mean pettiness and overreacting to little things. We make something out of nothing by turning a thing or a situation around to our advantage. Life experiences become grist for the mill. We can use every situation, no matter how painful or difficult, as a lesson from which to grow.

Today I will think of each difficult experience as grist for the mill. I will turn what happens around to my advantage by learning what I need to learn.

"Doubts are more cruel than the worst of truths."

Jean Baptiste Molière

Doubt is one of those cruel ghosts that haunts us day and night. It stalks us when we have a big day on the job and lurks over our shoulder when we're trying to make our primary relationships work.

Doubt is a roadblock; it prevents us from going far. Doubt keeps us from putting our all into our jobs and relationships. It even makes us unsure that we can grow spiritually. Recognizing doubtful thoughts for what they are — old tapes playing from the past — gives us the power to overcome them.

Doubt is conquered by self-confidence and faith. When we believe in ourselves and persist in our efforts, doubt is overpowered. We move forward, we participate in life.

Today I seek truth and escape from the clutches of doubt. Knowing that what I find from my persistence cannot be any worse than doubt keeps me ever self-confident.

"One day at a time! It's a wholesome rhyme;
a good one to live by, a day at a time."

Helen Hunt Jackson

No matter how hard life gets we always have
solace in the phrase, "One day at a time." When
life's burdens are too much to bear, when we
struggle with peril and indecision and overresponsibility, this one phrase can help us navigate through the sea of emotional turmoil. We
take only this second, this moment, this hour.
We live our lives now and we make it through
each day, one by one. This simple phrase releases us from immobilization and we always
work it through with ease one step at a time.

Today I live by the mottoes "One day at a
time" and "Easy does it." These simple re-
minders help me work through all tasks that
befall me.

"No one means all he says, and yet very few say all they mean, for words are slippery and thought is viscous."

Henry Brooks Adams

Spiritual growth means total commitment to our integrity. Even when we know we can get away with dishonest behaviors, small as they may be, we find our integrity at work. No one but us will ever be hurt by the little white lie that we told but we must live with ourselves. Lack of integrity hurts our spirit more than anything else. When we are not true to ourselves, we're living a life of hypocrisy, not integrity.

Today I ask myself, "Do I preach one thing and secretly do another?" As I look at even the smallest actions, I distinguish hypocrisy from integrity.

"Who lives content with little, possesses everything."

Nicolas Boileau-Despreaux

We have lost touch with our real selves, so we spend the greater part of our lives searching outside of ourselves for whatever will make us whole. Many times we expect our lover or spouse to make us complete. Sometimes we use work, drugs or food to fill the empty spot.

Fulfillment is not co-dependence. Nothing and no one outside of ourselves can make us finished. The key to fulfillment is in changing our erroneous thinking by understanding that we are already finished and complete, just as we are. We need simply live this belief for fulfillment to come.

Today I no longer look for something or someone to make me feel complete. I am at peace within myself.

"I was angry with my friend: I told my wrath, my wrath did end. I was angry with my foe: I told it not, my wrath did grow."

William Blake

There's nothing comparable to having other people love us unconditionally through thick and thin. Friends who can do this are like diamonds in the rough.

Friendships develop when two people open themselves enough to create a two-way relationship. We must let our friends see us without masking our real selves and agree to love them unconditionally when they reveal themselves to us.

Today I create new relationships or strengthen old ones by accepting my friends unconditionally and by letting my real self shine through for them.

"Forgiveness is the attribute of the strong."

Mahatma Gandhi

Holding on to our emotions when someone hurts, embarrasses or rejects us erodes the human spirit and damages growth. Forgiveness rids us of hurt and frees us to make decisions about our actions rather than allowing events to make decisions for us. Forgiveness makes us strong because we think and feel independently of the painful situation. Forgiving ourselves and others keeps us steady on the spiritual path, headed forward.

Today I ask for strength to practice forgiveness while maintaining my own sense of selfworth. Inspiration from my Higher Power will help me stand like a giant oak.

"Whatever with the past has gone, the best is always yet to come."

Lucy Larcom

We may find ourselves dwelling on the past because it takes away some of the painful present or our apprehensions of the future. It is an escape from facing life. Our past is over with and done. Staying stuck in the past stymies our forward movement and disconnects us from our lives. As long as we concentrate on the past, we have nothing new to live. Our lives ended years ago.

Turning toward the present brings hope and optimism. The good old days are here and now today.

Today I live in the present rather than dwell in the past. I am living the good old days today with gusto and growing from who I used to be.

"Most folks are as happy as they make up their minds to be."

Abraham Lincoln

How can we dwell on happiness when we have so much strife at work and disharmony at home? The answer is, "easily." We *have* the choice of where we want to put our thoughts. We can decide that we will give happiness equal time with despair. The dualities of joy and sadness, hate and love, right and wrong, good and evil are part of life's total package. By dwelling on joy, happiness, love and good we treat ourselves to a more balanced, self-satisfying experience of life.

Today I give the positive dualities in life equal time. Rather than dwelling on the pessimistic, I will concentrate on the optimistic.

"If you want to be respected by others, the great thing is to respect yourself."

Fyodor Dostoyevsky

Many of us have been taught that self-sacrifice is a great virtue. But always putting ourselves last and down is just as detrimental to the soul as always putting ourselves up and first.

When we accept deep within ourselves that we are our own best friend who deserves life's best, we live more fully. When we treat ourselves with the same love and respect, kindness and consideration we give those we care about, we treat ourselves to the grand prize rather than the consolation prize.

Today my well-being is enhanced because I treat myself with the same love, consideration and respect I give others. I am beginning to think of myself as a grand prize winner.

"When you're green, you're growing. When you're ripe, you rot."

Ray Kroc

Triumph comes not through superiority and false pride but through humility and compassion. Through negotiation, compromise and pride in someone else's accomplishments, we achieve the highest peaks of humanness. Admitting when another's idea works better than our own allows us to live with honor, honesty and humility.

Triumphs are merely road markers on life's journey. When we think of our triumphs as arrivals, we stop growing. Are we still green and growing? Or are we rotting on the vine?

Today I revel in the triumphs of my colleagues, for I know that their successes are my own. When I express pride and joy in their happiness, I receive the benefits of these good feelings a thousandfold.

*"Love consists in this, that two solitudes pro-
tect and touch and greet each other."*

Rainer Maria Rilke

The good feelings we get from doing little
things for others outweighs the good deed itself. Self-gratification comes from giving freely
and fully out of love and desire to share. Sharing and doing kind deeds are not done with
expectations. They are given freely from the
heart. We give because it feels natural and right.
We have taken our minds off our own troubles.
Self-pity and self-isolation no longer dominate
our thoughts.

*Today I will perform an act of kindness for
someone else. I rid myself of self-seeking and
self-centered thoughts by thinking of others
for a change.*

"When one devotes oneself to meditation, mental burdens, unnecessary worries, and wandering thoughts drop off one by one; life seems to run smoothly and pleasantly."

Nyogen Senzaki

Finding and living a spiritual life nurtures all our inner needs. Our spiritual awakening makes us feel centered, grounded and self-confident. Through self-examination, meditation and prayer we become connected with the past, present and future through a Higher "Knowing" — one that knows who we are, where we are and where we are headed. We put our lives in those hands and allow our Higher Power to guide us in the right direction.

Today I seek through prayer and meditation to improve my relationship with my Higher Power. I pray for continued knowledge of this Power's will for me and power so that I can carry that out.

"Plodding wins the race."

Aesop

Slowing down the pace of our lives is not easy with the demands of our jobs and families. There are never enough hours in the day to finish everything that needs to be accomplished. When we are consumed by a hurried lifestyle, we lose touch with who we are and we miss our lives along the way.

We can make a conscious effort to slow down the pulse and rhythm of our lives by talking slower, eating slower and driving slower. Caught in traffic or in a slow-moving line, we know the universe is telling us to slow down. We can seize these moments of waiting for spiritual reflection and replenishment.

Today I will build time for me into my daily life. I feel renewed as I quietly sit, reflect and pay attention to my inner self.

"Society is filled with invitations to be co-dependent. And, if we don't get invited, we may invite ourselves."

Anne Wilson Schaef

A colleague makes an unreasonable request and we say no. We put limits on a friend's tendency to take advantage. We refuse to bail out a loved one from a predicament resulting from repetitive dysfunctional behaviors. We feel a tinge of guilt, but we hold to our convictions.

When we live our lives first and foremost for ourselves as we do what we believe to be right, we have broken through the bonds of co-dependency.

Today I follow my convictions. I do what I believe to be right and live my life for myself rather than for others.

"It is better to wear out than to rust out."

Richard Cumberland

We are constatnly barraged with the message that excessive work is acceptable and preferable. We are applauded for abusive work habits and chronic overachieving. Compulsive working is counterproductive because it encourages self-neglect and co-dependency. We are spiritually strengthened by the knowledge that we do not have to be slaves to work. As we put our lives in order, we carve out time for the other important areas of our lives.

Today paying attention to my spiritual self, my family and my friends makes me whole and well-rounded. By nurturing my personal needs, I am more productive on the job.

"My life is a torn book. But at the end a little page, quite fair, is saved, my friend, where thou didst write thy name."

Edward Robert Bulwer Lytton

Real friends stand by us through good and hard times. Sometimes they are so loyal that we may take them for granted. Perhaps we use and abuse our friends without even realizing it. How do we treat our friends? Do we show them that we treasure and appreciate them in our lives? Or do we take them for granted?

Friendship involves receiving and giving. We can ask ourselves whether we are givers or takers in our friendships.

Today I am grateful for my friends. I will touch the hand of another today without thinking about what I need from them.

"Life is in your hands. You can select joy if you want or you can find despair everywhere you look."

Leo Buscaglia

We become so accustomed to grabbing onto others' pain and hurt that we miss riding our own wave of joy. Regardless of what happens in the hustle and bustle of daily life, we always have the choice of radiating joy. We don't wait for someone else to be joyful before we allow ourselves to express it. We don't have to have a reason to be joyful. We can simply choose it, regardless of the moods of those around us. Joy is all around us and within us. All we have to do is connect with it.

Today I feel joyful within. I will look for joy, feel joy and radiate joy to others. No matter what happens at the office or at home, I am joyful.

"There is no disappointment we endure one-half so great as that we are to ourselves."

Philip James Bailey

Many of us waste so much time and energy trying to be in control that we constantly create disappointments for ourselves. When we overstep our bounds with our controlling ways, our interference often goes against the grain of the universal rhythm. Once we get over the disappointment of our powerlessness and accept life as it is, it is impossible for us to disappoint ourselves.

Today I face the major disappointment that I am powerless. Accepting this fact keeps me from ever being a disappointment to myself again.

"It is easy enough to be pleasant, when life flows by like a song. But the man worthwhile is one who will smile, when everything goes dead wrong."

Ella Wheeler Wilcox

Where do we start when the spirit and mind are not in harmony? Acting "as if" we are the way we want to be eventually changes our attitudes to the way we want them to be. Sometimes it is necessary to start with our behavior to get our spirit to follow suit. Acting "as if" jumpstarts our heart and helps us turn blue moods and sour attitudes into more positive mental outlooks. We can create how we want to feel by acting "as if."

Today if I feel blue or have a sour attitude, I will act "as if" to change them to a more worthwhile mood. I can create how I feel and I am responsible for these feelings.

"No man, for any considerable period, can wear one face to himself, and another to the multitude, without finally getting bewildered as to which may be the true."

Nathaniel Hawthorne

Some of us learn to parrot the words of spiritual growth and easily advise others who have lost their way. But spiritual growth is more than spouting words and phrases that sound impressive. It means translating these words into action, practicing what we preach. When we internalize a program of spiritual recovery, we quietly live it by example. We don't have to flaunt it; others see it through expression in our daily lives.

Today I examine my life to make sure I'm not all words and no action. I practice what I preach.

"Our real blessings often appear to us in the shape of pains, losses and disappointments; but let us have patience, and we soon shall see them in their proper figures."

Joseph Addison

As we grow in our spiritual development, we change the way we look at the world. We see more beauty than flaws, more hope than despair. We see blessings and constructive outcomes even in loss and disappointment.

We have learned that we can create a happy life simply by changing our mental outlook. This small grain of knowledge empowers us to change our whole existence from helplessness to empowerment.

Today I take a positive view of my life. On other days when things look bleak, I simply change the blurry lens through which I view the world.

"The body travels more easily than the mind, and until we have limbered up our imagination we continue to think as though we had stayed home. We have not really budged a step until we take up residence in someone else's point of view."

John Erskine

Sometimes to truly grow, it helps to see the world from someone else's point of view. We draw a lot of erroneous conclusions about people and events when we don't consider other viewpoints. Empathy and understanding increase our sensitivity to others and help us not to be so quick to judge. It liberates our minds from narrow, negative thinking.

Today I limber up my mind by considering the angles others may take of situations. I keep my thinking wide and positive for the best results in my own growth.

"Envy comes from people's ignorance of, or lack of belief in, their own gifts."

Jean Vanier

Envy is a destructive force. It comes from a lack of appreciation for our own lives. Envy concentrates on our lack and discontent. Those of us who constantly compare our lot to another's and feel cheated by what we see, create a pit of despair.

As long as we compare ourselves to everyone we know or meet, we are stuck. The way to win is to value and affirm our own gifts. Give thanks for what we do have. Rejoice in our own uniqueness and talents. Self-satisfaction comes from appreciating what we have, not from wanting what others have.

Today I free myself from envy. I am aware of and believe in the value of my own life just as it is.

"Better to put a strong fence 'round the top of the cliff than an ambulance down in the valley."

Joseph Malins

Life would run more smoothly if we accepted it as it is rather than trying to make it the way we want. Sometimes this means going against old fears and insecurities and using courage to face life. But we cannot change the rules. As long as we try, we only avoid or postpone situations that must be dealt with eventually. We mustn't be afraid to face life as it is. We conserve more energy, lead a more fulfilled life and accomplish more with less frustration and greater ease in the long run.

Today I take life the easy way, the way it was meant to be. I accept people and events as they are, not as I want them to be.

"The tense American nerve relaxed, I lived with a gray quietness that let the mind grow inward like a root."

Paul Engle

Fast living is a habit that we get into without thinking. We can accept our quick-step society and participate in it without letting it monopolize our time and thoughts. We can develop healthy habits that keep us attuned with our inner selves. Special times to pamper ourselves, idle moments with no objectives to accomplish and deep meditation to connect with our Higher Power help us to live in the accelerated world with balance and serenity.

Today I keep attuned to my inner self. This enables me to participate in the fast-track world with serenity and fulfillment.

"All habits gather by unseen degrees — as brooks make rivers, rivers run to seas."

John Dryden

Our habits slowly mount up over time to make us who we are. Some are positive and some are negative. We can ask ourselves, "Are our habits taking us into rough waters and wild rapids? Or are they carrying us into calm and serene seas?"

Habits are made, and they can be broken. Each opportunity we have to break a bad habit puts us further on our spiritual path. Spiritual progress begins with the breaking of just one unhealthy habit that, when multiplied, yields a total healthy person.

Today I will think about my habits. I will think about which ones need breaking and which ones need developing.

"A fault confessed is more than half amended."

Sir John Harington

To advance in our personal healing, we complete the task of tying up loose ends. One approach to resolving past incompletions is to make a list of all persons with whom we have unfinished business and to make amends to them all. We shed long-held feelings, clear the air of misunderstanding and are better prepared to continue our spiritual journey. Wiping the slate clean gives us more energy for living life in the present.

Today I resolve old loose ends that have stockpiled. I resolve to amend my wrongdoings as they occur instead of leaving them for the future.

"The ability to simplify means to eliminate the unnecessary so that the necessary may speak."

Hans Hofman

The compulsive need to overdo is overpowering. When work at the office is done, it manifests itself in doing things around the house or planning other chores to do in the future.

We can surrender the urge to overdo and overwork to our Higher Power. We can simplify our lives by adding quiet periods of contemplation. As we give up the need to control our compulsive "busy-ness," our Higher Power brings us serenity and restores our peace of mind.

Today I surrender my overpowering urge to overdo because I cannot control it. I ask my Higher Power to take control and to let calm descend upon me.

"In public we say the race is to the strongest; in private we know that a lopsided man runs the fastest along the little side-hills of success."

Frank Moore Colby

The daily rat race to get ahead can make us lopsided. We strive to prove our self-worth in all efforts, and everything and everyone become a standard against which we measure our egos. Our way of doing something is *the* way. We amplify the triumphs of others into defeat for ourselves.

Becoming spiritually centered balances the need to compete and prove ourselves. Letting our human spirit shine through puts us on top.

Today I do not allow the rat race to make me lopsided. I find success in the world of competition and in my spiritual centeredness.

"Nothing is a greater impediment to being on good terms with others than being ill at ease with yourself."

Honoré de Balzac

We are unconsciously attracted to people who have the very co-dependent traits we are trying to shed. We merge our needy lives so tightly that we relinquish all sense of independence and individuality.

In spiritual progress we are no longer hooked by those who need us to make them feel whole. And our own neediness is satisfied by our inner healing.

Today I am not attracted to neediness in others and no longer give off needy signals to them. All human needs are satisfied by a deeper inner force beyond human capacity.

"Blisters are a painful experience, but if you get enough blisters in the same place, they will eventually produce a callus. That is what we call maturity."

Herbert Miller

Many of us feel vulnerable and afraid from time to time. We feel childlike inside. We even think and act like children. Sometimes we feel the helpless feelings of the child and forget that we are competent adults.

These thoughts, feelings and actions are governed by our inner child. Recovery empowers us with mature adult competence to calm fear, soothe hurt and give reassurance from abandonment. We trace the source of our fears to childhood and heal the feelings.

Today I nurture the needs of my inner child. Connecting with my mature adult gives me the comfort and security to satisfy all my needs.

"The real voyage of discovery consists not in seeking new landscapes but in having new eyes."

Marcel Proust

As we start to heal, we do not deliberately cause confusion just to be hostile. But as we get healthier, we begin to assert our needs. Speaking up for ourselves breaks old established patterns. Co-workers, loved ones and friends who are not used to our standing up for what we want may be somewhat surprised, even shaken by our change. The boat sways, rocks and might even sink. Those around us may reel from the change in us.

We don't have to let others' discomfort cause us to back down. The rocking boat will stabilize on its own as will everyone affected by it.

Today I don't worry about rocking the boat. I do not sacrifice my self-esteem so that others can have their way.

"Always vote for a principle, though you vote alone, and you may cherish the sweet reflection that your vote is never lost."

John Quincy Adams

We all must learn to give and take and to compromise. But we don't have to compromise who we are. When we're constantly giving in relationships and people are constantly taking, it's time to bring give and take into balance.

In healthy give and take relationships we do not compromise our inner selves. We can be open to flexibility and others' needs without sacrificing our honor and integrity.

Today I am willing to give and take. But I am not willing to give up my innermost self, my most cherished possession.

"The time which we have at our disposal every day is elastic; the passions that we feel expand it, those that we inspire contract it; and habit fills up what remains."

Marcel Proust

Living our lives planned to the split second allows no room for the unexpected events that befall us from time to time. Planning our days by building in time cushions absorbs the shock when something goes haywire. It reduces stress and keeps our outlook fresh. Cushioning our lives gives us space to stretch and breathe so that we can take a more human pace and be more flexible and spontaneous from moment to moment.

Today I build shock absorbers into my schedule. When the unexpected does occur, I handle it with calm and skill.

"The relation between superiors and inferiors is like that between the wind and the grass. The grass must bend when the wind blows over it."

Confucius

When we look at the relationship between the wind and grass, we can ask ourselves if we are in relationships where we're always the grass, blown about by others' wants and whims. Do we feel as if we're always underfoot?

We have a choice. We don't have to make ourselves inferior to others. We can care and love ourselves so that we are on an equal plane with others. Once we begin to love and care for ourselves, others will love and care for us too.

Today I blow with the wind. I treat myself with equality, not inferiority.

"You and I are but a pair of infinite isolations, with some fellow islands a little more or less near us."

William Makepeace Thackeray

There is no greater void than feeling isolated. We can feel cut off from people amid a swarm of shoppers or a stampede of morning commuters. Isolation often grips us when we are already low, making us feel apart from the human race.

We are not alone. Isolation is not a reality; it is but a feeling that will pass as we break through the bonds of co-dependency. Consolation comes in remembering the truth and using our tools for spiritual healing.

Today I know that even though I feel isolated, it is a feeling that will run its course. I am as much a part of the human race as anyone. I am not alone with my feelings.

"I think people ought to fulfill sacredly their desires. And this means fulfilling the deepest desire, which is a desire to live unhampered by things that are extraneous, a desire for pure relationships and living truth."

D. H. Lawrence

We don't own anyone or anything. In truth the only possessions we have are ourselves. Recovery teaches us to own our thoughts, feelings and behaviors whether right or wrong. Once we learn to do this, we have the most cherished possession of all — pure relationships and living our lives with truth and integrity.

Today I own my thoughts, feelings and actions. I treat others as separate human beings, not as objects of ownership.

"We put up with being surpassed more easily than being equalled."

A. Vinet

Sometimes life is about yielding to other viewpoints altogether. And sometimes it's about surrendering our self-will, admitting to our powerlessness.

Surrender is relating to others on an equal basis; submission is relating to others from an inferior position. We surrender our combative attitudes without submitting to domination or mistreatment. We continue to assert our beliefs and keep our self-respect while opening ourselves to other opinions.

Today I am learning the difference between surrender and submission. I will work on knowing when to surrender and when not to submit.

"To know what you prefer instead of humbly saying amen to what the world tells you you ought to prefer, is to have kept your soul alive."

R. L. Stevenson

We are not Siamese twins. Although we always need the love and help of others, we don't have to lose ourselves in their love and help. We are independent human beings, physically as well as spiritually. We have our own separate thoughts, feelings and actions. Spiritual healing is about keeping them separate, standing on our own feet and making our own decisions. We keep ourselves physically and emotionally alive through independence.

Today I am not physically and emotionally dependent on someone else. I have my own mind, body and spirit and can use them to my best advantage.

333

"Absolute rules are a device of cowardice to escape the difficulty of decision when an exceptional case occurs. A consistent refusal is always easier than an occasional compliance."

John Stuart Blackie

Sometimes we manage our personal lives as we do our business calendars. What insecurities do we hide behind when we need to order and plan our lives like a blueprint for a skyscraper? Why are we afraid to loosen up and live our lives moment to moment? Miracles happen unplanned and when we least expect them.

Today I loosen my life by deliberately introducing flexibility and spontaneity into it. As I make small changes, I open all sorts of new possibilities for personal growth.

"He works and blows the coals and has plenty of other irons in the fire."

Aristophanes

Nothing ever moves fast enough for those of us on the go. We are always struggling against the limits of time.

Outer distractions keep us off course and disoriented. Our focus on performing trivial tasks prevents us from dealing with the truly important issues in our lives. These compulsions distract us from our inner selves that, when nurtured, enable our lives to run smoothly. Inner reflection keeps us confident, clear and headed in the right direction.

Today I do not allow worldly distractions to steer me off the course of my spiritual trip. The Power within me is my steward. When I get confused or lose the way, my Inner Power keeps me pointed in the direction I need to go.

"What you keep to yourself you lose; what you give away you keep forever. What is the good of hoarding your money? Death has another key to your safe."

Axel Munthe

There comes a point in our healing where we want to return what we have received to the universe. We give freely of ourselves, not out of obligation, but out of love.

We connect from the heart, instead of just from the head. We share our spiritual growth with others and help them transform their own lives while their message spiritually strengthens us. We carry our message by word and example in all our daily affairs.

Today I live my life in ways I have been shown through my spiritual healing. I practice these principles and shine as an inspiration to others.

"There's no point in burying a hatchet if you're going to put up a marker on the site."

Sydney Harris

Sometimes we pretend to forgive but continue to carry old resentments and self-pity. When we harbor anger and resentment, we literally turn them inward upon ourselves where they do harm to us emotionally and physically. They stand in the way of our healing process and keep us stuck in misery and defeat.

We set ourselves free by releasing destructive feelings and forgiving ourselves and the wrong-doers. Turning our anger into love and forgiveness unblocks our spiritual path.

Today I inventory old feelings and release the ones that I still clutch. I bury the hatchet once and for all and set myself free.

"To know oneself, one should assert oneself."
                                    Albert Camus

As we progress in our spiritual travels, our attempts to become more assertive often teeter between aggressiveness and permissiveness. When we are aggressive, we steamroll over others in the face of opposition to ensure our needs and rights. When we are passive, we let others thrust their needs and rights upon us.

In recovery we don't seek power over others or allow others to force their power on us. By finding the middle ground of assertiveness we empower ourselves in a healthy way.

Today I will assert myself when necessary. But I will not confuse standing up for myself with depriving others of their rights or letting them deprive me of mine.

"The good die young — because they see it's no use living if you've got to be good."

John Barrymore

Many of us are people pleasers. We're still trying to be a good boy or a good girl so that everybody will love us and no one will ever reject us again. The compulsive need for approval comes from our upbringing in dysfunctional families.

We don't have to let messages from our inner child that directed our behavior as children direct us as grown-ups. We can make mature decisions that are right for us, whether or not others approve. Our goodness is defined by our own conscience and values.

Today I do not let childish messages guide my adult mind. My goodness as a human doesn't depend on the acceptance or approval of someone else.

"One man gets nothing but discord out of a piano; another gets harmony. No one claims the piano is at fault. Life is about the same. The discord is there, and the harmony is there. Study to play it correctly, and it will give forth the beauty; play it falsely, and it will give forth the ugliness. Life is not at fault."

Ninon de L'Enclos

Only by looking within and understanding ourselves can we ever understand the world and people in it. Harmony and oneness must be found within first. Harmony with others follows. It all starts with us.

Today I work in harmony with the world by finding it within myself first. I am seeing the world more positively and everything in it looks brighter.

"Pain is subtle. He has cold grey fingers. His voice is hoarse from crying and screaming."

Ruth Gendler

Many of us live with old pain from long ago that we re-enact within us. We may relive hurtful memories or still feel the pain of unresolved emotions. We have new pain too that seems to find us at every turn.

In recovery we learn how we unconsciously create new pain from old. We can never escape or eliminate pain from our lives. But as we heal, we discover how to live with pain, to find meaning in it and to use it to our advantage.

Today I stop running from pain but I also stop creating new pain out of the old. As I learn to live with pain, I experience it less and less.

"Most people don't care where they're going as long as they're in something that gets them there in a hurry."

Andy Rooney

Some of us do too much. By overdoing for tomorrow, we miss the here and now. In addition to our jobs, we busy ourselves caring for others perhaps more than we do for ourselves. When there's nothing to do, we manufacture something. We clean closets or pull weeds to keep busy. We leave the time for play and spirituality at the bottom of the list and we're always tired and unhappy.

Where are we going? Nowhere without some fun thrown in. Life is meant to be enjoyable too.

Today I experience enjoyment with a capital "E." I take time off from doing to play and enjoy.

"The most satisfying thing in life is to have been able to give a large part of oneself to others."

Pierre Teilhard de Chardin

Sharing ourselves in relationships is a problem for many of us from dysfunctional homes. We often get confused between setting boundaries and shutting others out. Boundaries define how far we go; barricades prevent us from going anywhere.

In recovery we are able to share ourselves as we genuinely are and to trust enough to remove barricades.

Today I am learning to remove barricades and erect boundaries. I am learning also to share myself and to express intimacy in a healthy way.

"If one advances confidently in the direction of his dreams, and endeavors to live the life which he has imagined, he will meet with a success unexpected in common hours."

Henry David Thoreau

Success is built on competition. We can become so consumed with achieving success that we drown in competition. The real success in life is not measured by how much we accomplish but by *how* we accomplish it. On our way to the top of the success ladder, our spiritual well-being is enhanced when we also rejoice in the successes of others. Living our lives with integrity and honor, we achieve the greatest success of all.

Today I think about what success means to me and how I achieve that success.

"Yes, an' no, an' mebbe, an' mebbe not."

Edward Noyes Westcott

Being indecisive leaves us floundering until decisions are eventually made for us by someone else or by chance. Taking action and making sound decisions for ourselves is a big part of being responsible for our spiritual healing. When we leave decisions to other people and situations, we lose our power and make ourselves victims. What action can we take today to empower ourselves that we have left to another person or situation?

Today I make decisions on all matters on which I have been floundering. I reclaim the power in my life by taking action on matters I have left to chance.

"The journey of a thousand miles begins with one step."

Lao Tzu

As the business world of machines moves faster, we try to keep up with their frenzied pace. But we are not machines; we are human beings. When we push our engines too far and too fast, we burn out.

We can ask ourselves what we are racing from: hurtful feelings, intimacy, fears of rejection and abandonment or feelings of low self-worth that are too painful to confront? Spiritual enlightenment brings us new and different ways of thinking about our actions. The rat race is won when we begin our spiritual journey with just one pace.

Today I reflect on hurrying. I look underneath my busy life and ask if I'm running from something I need to face.

"Nothing seems to me of the smallest value except what one gets out of oneself."

Oscar Wilde

When we look underneath the reasons for our clinging to others and our need to stay busy, we discover that we're often reliving childhood relationships many times over. Perhaps we continue to get involved in relationships with those who emotionally reject us.

Once we resolve the old feelings, we heal our compulsive need for love and approval. We start with accepting ourselves first. As we truly fall in love with ourselves, addictive relationships and chronic overachieving melt away.

Today I break the cycle of addictive relationships and overachieving. My value as a human being begins with me today through my own self-acceptance and self-love.

"If you miss the first buttonhole, you will not succeed in buttoning up your coat."

Goethe

If we want to get somewhere, we don't sit down. We take action and move. We take the path that is open to us. Healing comes from action, not lethargy. We must button the first button-hole to button our coats. Nothing ventured, nothing gained. Spiritual growth often means leaving ourselves vulnerable, facing the risk of criticism and going against fear.

We can risk being called "silly," being contradicted or being criticized but the risk makes us stronger. Let's dare to heal ourselves today by taking a new course of action.

Today I am open to positive change. I am not afraid to face risks that can lead to personal growth.

"I would rather sit on a pumpkin and have it all to myself than be crowded on a velvet cushion."

Henry David Thoreau

Some of us cling to people, things, old behaviors or bad habits. Clinging causes blurred and unhealthy boundaries and inability to separate one person from the other. It causes us to stifle each other, preventing our personal growth.

Healing means unraveling ourselves from addictive relationships, old habits and behaviors. It means feeling our own feelings, making our own decisions and being our own person.

Today I stop feeding off other people and things for my self-esteem. I am becoming my own person without clinging to anyone or anything for my needs.

"To know what you prefer, instead of humbly saying Amen to what the world tells you you ought to prefer, is to have kept your soul alive."

Robert Louis Stevenson

"Druthers" are something all of us could use more of. Too few of us know how to exercise our preferences because we have become so used to deferring to what others want. All of us have likes and dislikes and we can use our own minds to choose our preferences. There are times when we go along with the group and there are times when we assert our "druthers." Knowing what we prefer instead of letting the world tell us what to prefer keeps us growing in a healthy direction.

Today I am discovering my likes and dislikes. I can state my "druthers" without guilt when situations call for it.

"I always remember that I have everything I need to enjoy my here and now — unless I am letting my consciousness be dominated by demands and expectations based on the dead past or the imagined future."

Ken Keyes

There's no reason for us to be unhappy if we don't want to be. We have options and we can choose misery or happiness. Those of us who discover that we have chosen misery for the first part of our lives can choose happiness for the next half. It doesn't fall in our laps. It takes effort and self-discipline. It takes willingness to be open to new ways and a desire to grow. It takes hope and faith and some courage too. The choice is ours.

Today I am learning that I have choices I never realized. I am maximizing my options in favor of a happy and fulfilling life.

"Anyone who proposes to do good must not expect people to roll stones out of his way, but must accept his lot calmly if they even roll a few more upon it."

Albert Schweitzer

Our spiritual search fills us with life and a purpose for living. We open ourselves to whatever we encounter on our journey, no matter how rocky our path. We pry open our narrow minds that stifled our growth and gave us a one-sided and dysfunctional view of the world. We open our hearts to care for others and to let them care for us. In spiritual recovery, as we move from self-centeredness to self-love, we carry this love into our interpersonal relationships.

Today I think, feel and behave differently from the old me. I think about and do good things for others, even though my path may be rocky, without thought of what I will get in exchange.

"When we are spiritually enlightened, nothing changes, except the way we perceive, the way we use our minds."

William H. Houff

We find peace and serenity through solitude — a sanctuary that we create at home, in our office or in some other special place where we can be alone. Aloneness is a precondition for meditation and reflection on our lives and for healing to occur.

Those of us who walk a spiritual path are never truly alone because we have fulfilled that inner yearning and we enjoy being with ourselves. We are always in the company of our Higher Power.

Today I can get up 15 minutes earlier, go to bed 15 minutes late or take 15 minutes at lunchtime. I can always find time for spiritual contact.

"'Tis not my talent to conceal my thoughts, or carry smiles and sunshine in my face, when discontent sits heavy at my heart."

Joseph Addison

Many of our ways of communication get tangled and jammed. Perhaps we're afraid to be honest and direct with our feelings. So we either deny that they exist or we communicate them in subtle and indirect ways.

We may drop casual hints, use nonverbal behaviors, get someone else to speak for us or expect others to read our minds.

Recovery teaches us to express our emotions honestly and directly. Our candor with others ensures more open and strife-free relationships.

Today I untangle the ways in which I relate to people. I am kind, direct and honest in what I need to say and do.

"Equality is a quantitative term and, therefore, love knows nothing of it. Authority exercised with humility, and obedience accepted with delight are the very lines along which our spirits live."

Sinclair Lewis

Many of us act as if we're either inferior or superior to others. Both attitudes stem from insecurity. As long as we feel unequal to others, it's hard to act equally in relationships with them.

Getting along on an equal basis requires being genuine. We cast out old doubts and insecurities. We face ourselves honestly and discover that there is a universal human bond of feelings and thoughts.

Today I am breaking through feelings of inequality. I am thinking and feeling equal — not superior or inferior — to others in my life.

"Problems are the cutting edge that distinguishes between success and failure. Problems call forth our courage and our wisdom; indeed they create our courage and wisdom."

M. Scott Peck

One of the tools we use to break through our addictions and dysfunctions is boldness. Being bold means taking positive action. Perhaps we break old, unhealthy rules by which we've lived our lives. Or we take a different approach to a recurring problem. Boldness brings us spiritual strength to stand our ground, to defend our beliefs and needs.

Today I make my way through life boldly but gently. I boldly break unhealthy patterns that hold me back from my healing path.

"Today a friend wrote me, 'Do you think you are a mistake just because you made one?' "

Hugh Prather

When we make mistakes, we feel that *we* are the mistakes. If we do something wrong, shame and guilt surface as we confuse the action with ourselves and jam them all together in our minds. We feel that we are bad human beings.

That we *make* mistakes doesn't mean we *are* the mistake. In recovery we learn to untangle our deeds from our identities. We can separate wrongdoings from who we are and admit our downfalls without feeling ashamed or guilty.

Today I am learning to untangle my mistakes from myself. When I make mistakes, I admit the wrongdoing but continue to love and care for myself.

"Every man paddles his own canoe."

Frederick Marryat

We are always victimizing ourselves by living our lives for others and by putting ourselves into helpless positions. We become empowered once we admit our powerlessness and surrender to our Higher Power. Self-empowerment helps us stop feeling the emotions that belong to others and to feel our own emotions. We stop being responsible for others and become responsible for ourselves. We start feeling that we count for something and start standing up for ourselves.

Today I stop living my life for others and start living for myself. I am feeling empowered to take action and responsibility for making healthy changes in my life.

"Whether you realize it or not, there are no boundaries, but until you realize it, you cannot manifest it. The limitations that each one of us has are defined in the ways we use our minds."

John Daido Loori

We discover, in the healing process, that the self-fulfilling prophecy is alive and well in our heads. When we think and expect the best, we usually reap positive results. In contrast, thinking the worst will bring the worst. We learn that life is not all misery and drudgery. We don't live in a fantasy world of wonder and magic but we look for the best in all things.

Today I look at my life through realistic but optimistic eyes. I think positive thoughts, feel positive feelings, expect positive outcomes and serenity is mine.

"True progress consists not so much in increasing our needs as diminishing our wants."

Ivan Nikolayevich Panin

Those of us on a healing journey have exchanged material wants for spiritual ways. We are not controlled by material needs but by more substantive inner needs. We have discovered that we are more fulfilled by diminishing our wants, not increasing our needs. We are thankful for our families and loved ones and our special relationship with our Higher Power. We are grateful for all the new and healthy thoughts and feelings we have developed and for the happiness and fulfillment that have entered our lives.

Today I resist getting caught up in increasing my materialistic wants. Instead I diminish my wants and enjoy the rich blessings I already have.

"The way a chihuahua goes about eating a dead elephant is to take a bite and be very present with that bite. In spiritual growth, the definitive act is to take one step and let tomorrow's step take care of itself!"

William H. Houff

We live like a horse wearing blinders when we always focus straight ahead. Always setting our sights on the future and rushing forward, we miss some very important things along the way. Removing our blinders, we can pause to experience the things we would ordinarily miss along our journey. It lets us heal ourselves totally and feel life fully.

Today I remove the blinders from my life. I pause to experience my life openly and fully from every angle.

"No great thing is created suddenly, any more than a bunch of grapes or a fig. If you tell me that you desire a fig, I answer you that there must be time. Let it first blossom, then bear fruit, then ripen."

Epictetus

"HALT" stands for Hungry, Angry, Lonely or Tired. It is an alert signal for people in recovery, a gentle reminder to stop or slow down when one or a combination of the four are present. We can tuck this phrase away in our minds as a memory device to take it easy and one step at a time and let the healing process take a natural, even course of its own.

Today I remember to HALT when things become too much for me. I am healing myself, not all at once but gradually and step by step.

"We must all obey the great law of change. It is the most powerful law of nature."

Edmund Burke

We resist change, whether it is sought or imposed or happens by chance or design. Resistance keeps us stuck in the past and gives us a distorted image of today's reality.

Change is one of the few things in life we can count on. Dealing with our resistance and opening ourselves to whatever life brings helps us heal our present-day lives.

Today I am shedding resistance and surrendering to change. I know that it is the only thing I can be sure of, that it is healthy and that it is the way things are meant to be.

"Care is no cure, but rather corrosive, for things that are not to be remedied."

William Shakespeare

"Careaholics" are people addicted to taking care of others. They have a compulsive need to be overly responsible for other people and to overdo for them. Careaholics prevent others from taking care of themselves and from experiencing pain, hurt and other healthy emotions that can help them grow.

By detaching with love we can let others care for themselves and we can spend time caring for our own neglected lives.

Today I continue to love and care for others but I allow them to experience the outcome of their actions. I save some tender loving care for myself too.

"The largest part of mankind are nowhere greater strangers than at home."

Samuel Taylor Coleridge

It is not easy to face the past again. But as we confront the unhealthy family interactions with our healthy minds, we make headway in our personal growth. We discover how far we have come and how well we can cope. It builds our strength and faith. And it heals. We *can* go home again with a different outlook, different interpretations, rules and tools. We can face the battlefield once more and come out a winner for the rest of our lives.

Today I am gaining all the tools I need to face my past and put it to rest once and for all. I am becoming a different person, with a different mindset and a healthier and more confident outlook toward myself and life.

"What we call the beginning is often the end. And to make an end is to make a beginning. The end is where we start from."

T. S. Eliot

Today ends yet another year. We tend to think about the past year in review and to set resolutions for the new year to come. We are ending and beginning all at the same time. Today we can wipe the slate clean and begin anew.

The only way to finish a spiritual life is to be ever beginning it each day. There is always work to be done on ourselves.

Today as the year draws to an end, I make a new beginning in my spiritual journey. I am healthier and stronger than last year and am hopeful of even greater health and strength in the year to come.

INDEX